BULBS

THE PLANTER'S ENCYCLOPEDIA OF

BULBS

P E T E R   M c H O Y

Macdonald Orbis

A Macdonald Orbis BOOK

© Macdonald & Co (Publishers) Ltd 1988

First published in Great Britain in 1988
by Macdonald & Co (Publishers) Ltd
London & Sydney

A Pergamon Press plc company

British Library Cataloguing in Publication Data

McHoy, Peter, 1941–
The planter's encyclopedia of bulbs
1. Gardens: Flowering bulbs
I. Title
635.9′44

ISBN 0-356-15312-6

Filmset by Flair plan phototypesetting Ltd.

Printed and bound in Portugal by Printer Portuguesa

Editor: Jennifer Jones
Art Editor: Muffy Dodson
Designer: Judith Highton
Picture Research: Christina Weir

Macdonald & Co (Publishers) Ltd
Greater London House
Hampstead Road
London NW1 7QX

INTRODUCTION · 6

A·Z OF BULBS · 12

INTRODUCTION

GETTING THE BEST FROM BULBS

All the plants in this book have one thing in common: they have storage organs, which are commonly known as 'bulbs'. Only some of them are true bulbs (others have corms, tubers, or rhizomes), but they are usually loosely grouped under this general term because they can be bought from a bulb merchant. The box on page 9 explains the differences between the various terms, if you're not sure of them.

Most of the bulbs in this book are hardy, and will grow perfectly well even in cold parts of the country, but some of them are on the borderline of hardiness and it may be necessary to give them some winter protection; a few are usually grown as houseplants or greenhouse plants. We've also included a few that are popularly treated as houseplants, but relatively few of the plants in this book will be happy as permanent residents in the home.

It's fun to bring pots of bulbs into your home to bloom of course, and many kinds can be forced into early flower indoors – though in the case of hyacinths and tulips it's necessary to buy bulbs that have been specially treated (or 'prepared') if you want very early blooms.

BUYING BULBS

All the plants in this book should be available from commercial sources, though obviously stocks and availability of the less common types will vary from year to year. Most bulbs should be obtainable from garden centres and shops, or a good general bulb merchant. However, you may have to shop around for some of them – especially towards the end of the season. Mail order shopping has a lot to commend it. Provided you order early there should be a much wider choice than at a garden centre, and it is normally possible to obtain most of the bulbs you require from the comfort of your armchair.

A few of the less common species are available only from companies that specialize in uncommon bulbs, but we have indicated them where this is the case. Some of the rarer species and varieties are well worth searching out – growing something different is always fun, and it is nice to have a few plants in your garden that visitors are going to ask about.

Buying from shops does have advantages of course. If you tend to leave things until the last minute (or are simply impatient), you can decide on what you want in the morning and be planting that afternoon. Another big advantage is that you can see what you are buying. The text below should help you to identify the best bulbs and avoid the dubious ones.

Some of the plants mentioned on the following pages – crocosmias and dahlias, for example – can be bought as growing plants from nurseries and garden centres. Some, such as achimenes and caladiums, are sold as indoor pot plants, and this is often a convenient way of obtaining them if you've missed the planting time for the tubers.

CHOOSING BULBS

If possible, check bulbs before you buy them. It is not unusual to find some in a batch which show signs of disease, and you should be able to detect bulbs of poor quality. Not only is it a waste of money to buy these but you also run the risk of other bulbs in your garden becoming diseased.

Look for:

Firm bulbs, corms or tubers which are comparatively heavy for their size. In the case of true bulbs, the larger and heavier the bulb, the more likely it is to flower well. The same goes for corms, though 'depth' can also be important (a small thick gladiolus is likely to be better than a large flat one).

Large tubers do not necessarily perform better than smaller ones (assuming they are at least of flowering size). Large old tubers can be reluctant to sprout, and in the case of dahlias the finest exhibition flowers are often grown from cuttings that have no tuber at all when planted out.

Some bulbs, such as tulips, have a thin

Crocosmia × *crocosmiiflora* 'Citronella' (above) and *Dahlia* 'Ruwenzori' (below) are ideal for the summer border and will usually flower on into early autumn.

protective skin (the tunic), and whenever possible this should be intact. It is inevitable that there will be some damage to the tunic on most bulbs, but it is only likely to be detrimental if it is extensive.

Avoid:

Bulbs that have shrivelled, or those with soft areas, especially round the base or the neck.

Avoid any with signs of mould, no matter how small the area. If you notice aphids or other insects on the bulbs, it is best not to buy any bulbs from that batch.

PLANTING BULBS

Bulbs are amazingly tolerant. Although it is not to be recommended, if you plant them upside down many will probably come up the right way. (If you are in doubt about which is the top of an irregularly shaped tuber, try planting it on its side.) They will almost certainly grow if you plant them more deeply or shallowly than recommended, and you are almost sure of a dependable initial show even if the ground is impoverished and you don't add any fertilizer.

However, it is never a good idea to handicap any plant by not giving it the best start in life, so it is worth making a point of planting carefully.

Recommended planting depths are given for each entry in this book, but bulb sizes (and therefore planting depths) can vary between different species so it is useful to have a rule of thumb. Make the planting hole three times the depth of the bulb, corm or tuber – so that it is covered with soil to about twice its own depth.

When there are a lot of bulbs to be planted, it is tempting to rush the job and dig inadequate planting holes. If you use a trowel it is very easy to produce a tapering pocket, narrower towards the bottom, which leaves air beneath the bulb. Avoid this by making a straight-sided hole, or at least remove enough soil to ensure that there are no air pockets beneath the bulbs.

Most bulbs, but not all, prefer a well-drained soil. If yours is heavy, try to incorporate plenty of garden compost and a generous amount of coarse grit in the planting area. Books popularly recommend a handful of sand or grit in the planting hole, but if you overdo this there is the danger that the pocket of grit will simply act as a sump in which water will collect. Rotting caused by poor drainage is one of the most common causes of failure. It is better to improve drainage in the whole planting area than simply to use a handful of grit beneath individual bulbs.

Mixed hyacinths around a tree – bulbs usually look best planted in informal groups.

If a lot of bulbs have to be planted, it may be worth investing in a bulb planter. This tool takes out a core of soil (in the case of long-handled models, without too much bending), and speeds up the job considerably. The size of the hole it makes, however, cannot be varied and it is useful only if the bulbs are the right size for the hole. In the case of very tiny bulbs, when the hole will be much too large, you may be able to plant a small group of say three in the one hole.

Planters are often used to remove cores from the lawn where bulbs are to be naturalized, as it's then easy to replace the core and leave the grass relatively intact. But it is often easier, for small bulbs, to lift a small area of turf with a spade, scatter the bulbs, and then let the turf drop back.

Unless you are growing the bulbs as part of a formal bedding scheme, avoid planting in rows. Informal groups almost always look more attractive.

FERTILIZERS

True bulbs of flowering size already contain embryo flowers, so feeding them when you plant them will not make much difference to flowering performance (which is one reason why newly planted bulbs are so reliable, even in difficult positions). Bulbs planted in autumn may benefit from a dressing of a slow-acting fertilizer such as bonemeal, but avoid anything that will stimulate growth during the cold season. In spring it is worth applying a general balanced fertilizer over the area where summer-flowering bulbs have been planted.

True bulbs will flower with the minimum of feeding for the first year (assuming they are of flowering size), but decline will set in and the flowers will become smaller and sparser if the plants are not fed once the leaves are growing vigorously.

Plants that have tubers and rhizomes do not already have the embryo flowers when planted, so it is worth feeding them throughout the growing season (provided this does not stimulate growth during the cold months).

INCREASING YOUR STOCK

All types of bulbs are easy to propagate; because they are storage organs, they lend themselves to various forms of division. Many are also easy to grow from seed, although this is usually a slow method and therefore an option to consider only when you need a large number of plants.

True bulbs produce offsets (small bulbs) around the base of the parent bulb, which in turn grow into flowering-sized bulbs. This can lead to overcrowding in time and flowering can then begin to suffer. Flowers may become fewer or smaller. However, this natural method of division can be used for propagation. With many bulbs, such as daffodils, the offset bulbs can simply be pulled away from the parent and grown on

until flowering size is reached (which in some cases can be remarkably quickly). Often these will separate naturally when you lift the plant, or they can be separated with a sharp knife. If you do this, it is worth treating the cut area with a fungicide.

The rate and manner in which the offsets are produced affects the performance of the parent bulb. Daffodils, for instance, generally produce offsets without affecting the flowering power of the parent bulb immediately. This means that there are seldom 'off' years where the parent bulb has effectively finished useful flowering, but the offsets are not yet large enough to flower. *Iris danfordiae* is among the plants that split up into a lot of small bulbs with the parent bulb practically withering away. This means that there may be a 'blank' year or two while the offsets are becoming large enough to flower. Many large-flowered hybrid tulips also tend to divide into many small non-flowering offset bulbs, whereas some dwarf tulip species can be relied on to flower again the next year.

In either case, for propagation purposes the offset bulbs should be grown on for a year or two in a spare piece of ground until they approach the flowering size (the size of the parent bulb will give you a good idea of when a bulb is large enough to flower well).

BULB, CORM OR TUBER?

True bulbs consist of modified leaves which have become swollen food-storing scales. The bulbs are usually oval or pear-shaped in outline, and there is a clear basal disc from which the roots emerge.

If a bulb is cut in half, the layers or scales can be seen clearly, like an onion. Once the bulb is large enough to flower, the embryo flower shoot can be seen.

Corms are modified stems, and if you cut one in half it will look relatively solid, without regular layers or scales (although there may be a protective outer skin).

Stem tubers usually (but not always) grow at ground level. Tubers are usually

relatively irregular in outline, and the flesh is solid. Shoots arise from the top of the tuber and roots from the base. Tuberous-rooted begonias and cyclamens are examples of stem tubers.

Root tubers grow below ground, and the shoots arise from a piece of stem at the crown. They will not grow if individual tubers are severed without a small section of stem attached. Dahlias are root tubers.

Rhizomes are underground stems that grow horizontally along the surface of the soil, or beneath it – leaves grow from the sides or top, and roots from the base.

If old, established clumps are being divided, and you need only a few more plants, it should be possible to divide the clumps into sections with bulbs at various stages of development, so ensuring regular flowering from the beginning.

Lilies are unusual. Instead of layers of modified leaves being held closely together in an outer skin, they form distinct and separate fleshy 'scales' joined at the base. The best way to propagate them is to remove the scales, treat them with a fungicide and then pop them into a bag of damp perlite or vermiculite. Seal the bag and place it in an airing cupboard, or other warm place. Try to maintain a temperature of 20°C (70°F). If the warmth and humidity are adequate, small bulbs should form at the base of the scales, and these can be potted up in due course and grown on in a nursery bed until ready to be planted out.

A few bulbs form bulbils in the axils of the leaves. Some lilies are well known for this phenomenon. Remove the bulbils and plant them in trays of potting compost. When they are large enough set them out in the garden and grow them on for a year or two until flowering size is reached.

Corms produce cormlets around the baseplate. If an old corm that has flowered is lifted, you will see that a new one has formed on top of the old one, with masses of small cormlets around the edge. Remove the old withered corm, and replant the new one where it is to flower. The small cormlets can be saved and grown on for a season before being planted in their flowering positions.

Rhizomes and tubers can usually be divided with care to produce plants that will flower with the minimum of delay. Use a clean, sharp knife to cut the tuber or rhizome into sections. With root tubers, such as dahlias, each piece must have a section of the stem too if the plants are to grow. Stem tubers, such as tuberous-rooted begonias, still need careful division, as each segment should have an 'eye' (where the shoots arise).

Leaf and stem cuttings can also be used to propagate a few of the plants mentioned in this book: some begonias come easily from leaf cuttings and stem cuttings are used to propagate achimenes, for example.

USING BULBS AROUND THE GARDEN

Most bulbs are probably bought for spring bedding and for naturalizing in grass. But their scope goes much further. Summer borders can be enhanced by lilies, agapanthus, and crocosmias, to name but a few; in autumn colchicums, nerines and sternbegias can be used to bring pockets of colour to the garden just as everything else seems to be coming to an end.

Many of the smaller spring-flowering bulbs are excellent in containers such as windowboxes and troughs, but don't overlook some of the large and majestic summer-flowering bulbs for a large tub on the patio or perhaps in the conservatory. Crinums and agapanthus are ideal for this.

Rock gardens are an ideal home for many of the dwarf bulbs, many species of which grow naturally in rocky alpine conditions. But bold groups are essential if the tiny species

Nerine bowdenii (above) and *Sternbergia lutea* (below) will provide splashes of colour to the autumn garden.

are to be appreciated; a few crocuses or snowdrops will go almost unnoticed among the rocks and other plants, but a drift of them will be an eyecatching spectacle.

Although alpine enthusiasts are likely to be growing the rarer and more difficult plants in pots in a greenhouse or alpine house (a kind of greenhouse with particularly good ventilation), many of the dwarf bulbs, including some of the compact tulips, make ideal subjects to grow in pots for the greenhouse bench.

Try growing bulbs through ground cover such as ivy or even between and among heathers. They can bring colour at a time when the ground cover itself is looking weary, yet you are never left with bare ground when the bulbs have died down. Some of the dwarf and species daffodils are useful for this. Also, try the smaller and more delicate-looking species crocuses instead of the more commonly used dwarf

carpeters such as thyme.

The advantage of combining bulbs with ground cover is that it enables the bulbs to grow and multiply undisturbed, yet avoids leaving bare soil when the bulb foliage dies down. Besides the ground covers already mentioned, try ajugas, and *Vinca minor*. If you are growing taller plants such as lilies, try using ferns at ground level.

For a really adventurous use of bulbs, try creating a bulb bed. By planting only bulbs, and making sure there are species that flower at each season, it's possible to create an unusual and interesting corner of the garden. Although an ordinary bed of soil can be used, it is a good idea to grow them in a gravel bed – created by digging plenty of fine gravel or grit into the ground to improve drainage, and finishing with a layer of gravel at least 5cm (2in) thick. This will encourage less weed growth, and can actually make a more attractive feature out of the bed.

Tulipa greigii hybrid 'Gluck' – many dwarf tulips can be grown in pots.

A

ACHIMENES
(Hot water plant)

Achimenes are plants for the home or greenhouse, not for the garden. The name is probably derived from the Greek word *cheimaino*, meaning to suffer from cold, or to be tender. If they receive a severe chill during the growing season, it may be enough to stop growth.

Despite this drawback, achimenes are easy plants to grow if you can provide the right conditions, and they really do make rewarding pot plants.

Most mail-order bulb merchants and some seedsmen sell the rhizomes (technically, scaly tubercles), and there are achimenes specialists who offer a wide range of varieties. Don't expect to find the rhizomes widely available in garden centres, although you should be able to buy the growing plants in garden centres and florists.

Individual blooms are short-lived, but

▽ *Achimenes* 'Rumpelstiltskin'

there are usually plenty more to follow, with flowering extending from early summer until mid autumn.

Most varieties have pink or purple flowers, but there are lavenders, mauves, whites, and even a rare yellow.

HOW TO GROW

Achimenes are best grown in a greenhouse in a hanging basket, but they will also do well on a light window-sill indoors. If the light is too poor, the plant will become leggy and probably fail to flower well; yet direct strong sunlight through glass will probably scorch

the leaves, causing them to turn brown. Try to keep the temperature above 13°C (55°F), with moderate humidity.

Plant 10–20mm (½–¾in) deep in a lime-free compost, putting about three to five of the cone-like rhizomes into a 20cm (8in) pot. Water moderately until growth begins – using water that has had the chill taken off it will probably speed things along.

The young shoots are weak and wiry, and you can either let them trail over the edge of the pot or give them some support and train the plants into a more upright shape. Pinch out the tips of the young shoots to produce bushier plants.

If you live in a mild area you could grow them in a hanging basket outdoors, but only after careful hardening off.

Never let the compost dry out during the growing season, and give the plants a weak liquid feed once a month.

Once the plant ceases to bloom in the autumn, gradually withhold water, and cut off the stems when they have withered.

The rhizomes can be stored in dry peat in a frost-free place, but you can also leave them in the pots for the winter if this is more convenient.

PROPAGATION

Plant cuttings of young shoots, about 5cm (2in) long, in late spring; or divide and replant rhizomes in early spring. They multiply rapidly, and once the pots become overcrowded they will have to be divided and replanted anyway, making this is an easy and reliable method of propagation.

POPULAR SPECIES

The plants usually available are hybrids, derived from species from central America and Mexico. Specialist nurseries offer named varieties.

ACIDANTHERA

The name comes from the Greek *akis* (a point), and *anthera* (an anther).

This plant has had botanists disagreeing over its name almost since it was first introduced. At that time it was thought to be

Acidanthera bicolor murielae

a gladiolus and was given the name *Gladiolus murielae*; later it became an acidanthera but the name is still disputed. In catalogues you will still find it listed as an acidanthera, and the one form generally cultivated is usually sold as *A. bicolor* or *A. bicolor murielae*. Acidantheras look best in a herbaceous or mixed border.

HOW TO GROW

A warm, sunny spot is essential for good results. Plant out in late spring to a depth of about 10cm (4in), preferably in well-drained, gritty soil. Lift the corms in the autumn and store in a cool but frost-proof place until the following spring.

PROPAGATION

When lifting the corms, save the small cormlets that have been produced. Pot them up in early spring and grow on in a cold frame. Take in and store for the winter, and repeat the cycle a couple more times – by which time they should be large enough to flower in the autumn.

POPULAR SPECIES

A. bicolor murielae (Abyssinia). Fragrant, white, star-like flowers with a distinctive deep maroon blotch in the centre, in autumn. Sword-like leaves. 90cm (3ft).

AGAPANTHUS
(African lily, lily of the Nile)

The name agapanthus is derived from the Greek words *agape* (love) and *anthos* (flower).

Agapanthus would be more widely grown if

Agapanthus praecox orientalis 'Blue Pearl'

Agapanthus praecox praecox 'Albus'

they did not have the reputation for being tender. Some species certainly do need winter protection even in mild areas, but there are quite hardy species and strains that withstand a reasonable degree of frost and can be left outdoors for the winter in favourable regions. Even where the winters are too cold to leave them outdoors, they make magnificent tub plants that you can move into the greenhouse or conservatory for the winter.

Although agapanthus like warmth and sunshine, they also do well in front of shrubs, where they seem to appreciate the shelter provided. They can of course be planted in herbaceous borders, but they usually look most effective in drifts at the front of a sunny shrub border, or in containers, perhaps on a sunny patio.

Most agapanthus have rounded heads

composed of clusters of blue trumpet-shaped flowers, although there are white forms. Some species, with bold strap-like leaves, are evergreen.

▲ *Agapanthus* 'Headbourne Hybrid'

▼ *Agapanthus campanulatus*

They are commonly bought as growing plants from nurseries, but you can also buy the fleshy rhizomes from bulb merchants.

HOW TO GROW

If growing in a container, use a tub rather than a pot. Use a good potting compost, ideally with extra leaf-mould and sand added.

Plant firmly, and water freely from spring to autumn, feeding regularly until the plant has finished flowering. Don't repot until the plants seem to be bursting out of the container, as they generally flower best when the roots are restricted.

If planting in open ground, choose a warm, sheltered and sunny position if possible, and enrich the soil with plenty of garden compost or well-rotted manure first. Water freely in dry weather, especially for the first year after planting. Choose the hardiest kinds, and plant the crowns about 5cm (2in) below soil level.

Cut the flowering stems back to ground level once they have finished blooming, and in late autumn protect the crown with a 15cm (6in) layer of bracken, coarse sand, or pulverized bark. This can be removed in spring once the plants start to grow again.

PROPAGATION

Lift and divide the plants in early spring. After division the plants may need a season to settle down again before they resume flowering. Agapanthus can also be raised from seed. They will germinate quite easily if sown in warmth in mid spring. You will need to grow them on in a frost-free place for a couple of years, but many should have reached flowering size by the third year.

POPULAR SPECIES

A. africanus (*A. umbellatus*) (Cape Province, S. Africa). An evergreen species, but not really hardy. Deep blue flowers in mid and late summer. 60–75cm (2–2½ft).
A. campanulatas (Natal). Blue flowers in late summer. 75cm (2½ft) high.
A. 'Headbourne Hybrids' (garden origin). Some of the hardiest agapanthus. Spherical heads of pale blue to deep violet flowers. 60–75cm (2–2½ft).
A. praecox (E. South Africa). There are several sub-species, including *A. p. orientalis* (*A. orientalis*), with varieties in white and various shades of blue. 60–75cm (2–2½ft).

ALLIUM
(Ornamental onion)

The name 'allium' was originally used for garlic, but the name may have derived originally from the Celtic *all*, meaning pungent or burning; the foliage is likely to smell of onions if bruised.

Many members of this group are very decorative. They are also diverse in appearance and habit, with compact plants for rock gardens to giants of over 1.2m (4ft) for herbaceous borders. Most of them are easy to grow, with the smaller ones generally increasing rapidly, although there are many rare kinds, such as *A. altissimum*, for the specialist.

Most of the popular species flower in the spring or in summer, and it's not uncommon for them to be in bloom for about a month. Because of their long-lasting qualities, they are also popular

Allium albopilosum

Allium altissimum

Allium giganteum

Allium aflatunense

with flower arrangers as well as gardeners, especially with those interested in Japanese, freestyle and abstract arrangements. Some of them can be dried successfully and used in 'everlasting' decorations.

HOW TO GROW

Most alliums prefer well-drained soil in an open, sunny position. The soil does not have to be rich, and once established alliums will require little attention; it is best to leave the clumps undisturbed for as long as possible.

Plant alliums in the late autumn or in the spring, covering the bulbs with soil to about twice their own depth.

△ *Allium karataviense*

PROPAGATION

Lift and divide established clumps in early autumn. The largest bulbs can be replanted to form new clumps that should soon flower; the smaller bulbs can be grown on in a spare piece of ground.

Seed is a much slower method, but is useful if you require a large number of plants. Sow in a gritty compost in a cold frame in early or mid spring, and the following spring prick out the seedlings into small individual pots. Harden them off, plunge the pots outdoors for the summer, and overwinter in a frame. After another summer plunged in a spare piece of ground they should be ready for planting out.

POPULAR SPECIES

A. aflatunense (Central Asia). Large, round heads of purple-lilac star-like flowers in late spring. Strap-shaped leaves. 75cm (2½ft).
A. albopilosum (*A. christophii*) (Middle East). Large rounded heads of small, lilac-pink star-flowers in early summer. Strap-shaped leaves. 45cm (1½ft).
A. caeruleum (*A. azureum*) (Siberia). Small dense balls of sky blue flowers in early and mid summer. 45cm (1½ft).
A. cernuum (USA). Nodding mauve, rose, purple or white flowers, in summer. 46–60cm (1½–2ft).
A. flavum (S. Europe). Masses of glistening sulphur-yellow flowers in loose heads in mid

 Allium rosenbachianum

▽ *Allium moly*　　　　　　　　　　▽ *Allium neapolitanum*

Allium sphaerocephalum

summer. 30cm (1ft).

A. *giganteum* (Himalaya). Rounded heads of deep lilac flowers; 10cm (4in) or more across, in early summer. 1.2–1.5m (4–5ft).

A. *karataviense* (Turkestan). A large rounded head of pink or white flowers with crimson-tinted leaves. 23cm (9in).

A. *moly* (S. Europe). Bright yellow star-like flowers in loose heads, in early and mid summer. 30cm (1ft).

A. *narcissiflorum* (*Alps, Caucasus*). Pink bell-shaped flowers which bloom in early summer. 23cm (9in).

A. *neapolitanum* (Italy). White, lace-like, scented flowers, in late spring. Can be slightly tender; makes an effective pot plant for the greenhouse. 30cm (1ft).

A. *ostrowskianum* (A. *oreophyllum*) (Turkestan). Dwarf species; purple-pink flowers in late spring. 15cm (6in).

A. *rosenbachianum* (Central Asia). Large balls of rose-purple flowers, in late spring. The variety 'Album' has silvery-white flowers. 1.2m (4ft).

A. *roseum* (S. Europe). Soft pink, long-lasting flowers in late spring. 30–45cm (1–1½ft) high.

A. *siculum* (A. *nectaroscrodum*) (France, Sicily, Italy). An uncommon species with hanging, bell-like, green and maroon flowers; the form A.s. *bulgaricum* has larger, deep brown and blue-green flowers. Both species flower in the late spring and in early summer. 90cm (3ft) high.

Allium narcissiflorum

Allium oreophilum ostrowskianum

Allium ursinum

prefers shade. Can become invasive. 30–45cm (1–1½ft).

A. ursinum (Europe). This species has starry white flowers, which bloom in late spring. 30cm (1ft) high.

ALSTROEMERIA
(Peruvian lily)

Alstroemerias are perennials with fleshy, tuberous roots and a reputation for being difficult to grow. They are named after a Swedish botanist Baron Claus Alstromer

Alstroemeria hybrid

A. sphaerocephalum (W. Europe to Iran). Crimson-maroon heads, flowering in mid summer. 60cm (2ft) high.

A. triquetrum (S. Europe). Loose heads of slightly scented, nodding, green-and-white flowers on triangular stalks. This species

(1736–94), who was a friend of the great botanist Linnaeus.

Although not dependably hardy in cold areas, in the milder regions where the winters are not too severe they should overwinter without difficulty.

The clumps take a while to become established and can be rather disappointing in a herbaceous border at first, but massed together they make beautiful plants.

The tubers do not like being out of the ground for long, and although they can be bought as tubers, it is probably better to buy growing plants.

The prettily marked flowers usually appear in late spring and flowering can be expected to continue for a month. They are excellent for cutting, and are sometimes grown commercially as cut flowers.

HOW TO GROW

Plant the thick, finger-like tubers in spring, handling them carefully as they are brittle and break easily. Plant about 30cm (1ft) apart. Position the crown about 10cm (4in) below the surface, spreading out the roots carefully. Container-grown plants can be planted at any time during the growing

Alstroemeria ligtu hybrids

segments into 15cm (6in) pots, and grow on in a cold frame for a year before planting out after careful hardening off.

They can be raised from seed, but it isn't easy. Soak the seeds in tepid water for 12 hours before sowing in a temperature of about 24°C (75°F). After about a month try lowering the temperature to about 13°C (55°F). When the seeds eventually germinate, pot them up individually and grow them on in a cold frame. Plunge the pots up to their rims in soil for protection, and it may be necessary to insulate the frame in cold weather. Finally plant out when large enough after hardening off.

POPULAR SPECIES

A. aurantiaca (Chile). Trumpet-shaped, yellow and orange flowers on tall, leafy stems, in summer. 90cm (3ft).
A. ligtu hybrids (garden origin). These hybrids are noted for their good colour range, which includes shades of pink, orange, yellow, and flame. 60–75cm (2–2½ft) high.

AMARYLLIS

This genus, which takes its name from a shepherdess in Greek and Latin poetry, has just one species – *A. belladonna*. The species takes its name is from the Italian *bella* (pretty) and *donna* (lady) because, it is said, an extract from the plant was used as a cosmetic in the past to brighten the eyes.

The plant should not be confused with the hippeastrums, which look rather similar and have the common name name of amaryllis. Whereas hippeastrums (see page 89) are indoor plants, *A. belladonna* can be grown outdoors, albeit in a warm, sheltered position in mild areas. It's a useful, late-blooming plant, the flowers coming in early autumn and lasting for about three weeks.

HOW TO GROW

Grow in a sheltered position, perhaps at the foot of a warm, sunny wall. Early summer is usually the best time to plant, in well-drained soil enriched with plenty of garden

season, but they should grow more readily in the spring.

Grow in a rich, well-drained loam, in partial shade or filtered sunlight. Grow in colonies; isolated plants may require staking. Water freely, especially while the plants are becoming established, and give a dressing of a general fertilizer once a year soon after the shoots have emerged.

Do not cut too many stems for the house until the plants are well established, but dead-head regularly unless the seed is required. Cut the stems down to ground level in autumn once the leaves have turned yellow.

During the winter protect them with a thick layer of peat, bracken, pulverized bark, or even sand, for the winter.

PROPAGATION

Divide existing clumps, although they should be disturbed as little as possible. Pot up compost or well-rotted manure. The large bulbs should be covered with about 8–15cm (3–6in) of soil, spacing them about 25cm (10in) apart.

Dead-head as the blooms fade, and cut down the stem when flowering is over.

Mulch in spring and water regularly in summer. An annual dressing of a balanced fertilizer should be beneficial.

In all but the mildest districts, it is worth

Amaryllis belladonna

Anemone coronaria

protecting the crown in winter with a thick layer of pulverized bark, bracken, or peat.

PROPAGATION

Divide established clumps in early or mid summer, replanting the separated offsets immediately. Grow them on under glass in 12–15cm (5–6in) pots for a year before planting out. Offsets may take about three years to flower. The clump may take several years to flower again as it has been disturbed.

It is possible to increase the stock from seed, but you could have to wait up to eight years for the plants to flower.

POPULAR SPECIES

A. belladonna (South Africa and Namibia). The stiff stems are topped with clusters of bright pink flowers about 10cm (4in) across, in early and mid autumn, with no leaves. There is also a white form. 60–90cm (2–3ft).

ANEMONE

here are several suggested origins for the plant name; one is that it comes from the Greek *anemos* (wind) and *mone* (a habitation), as some species enjoy windy places. Others think it to be associated with the Greek god Adonis, whose spilled blood (legend says) produced *Anemone coronaria* when he died in battle.

The popular florist's anemone is one of the best-known tuberous kinds, but there are several very useful rock garden species too. All are worth growing, and the florist's type is excellent for cutting; with careful cultivation and special techniques, it's possible to have these plants in bloom at almost any month of the year.

Not all anemones have tuberous roots; some border kinds have fibrous roots, but these are not included in this book. Most

Anemone blanda 'Bridesmaid'

tuberous anemones flower in spring, though the florist's strains can be induced to flower out of season.

The florist's anemones, such as 'St. Brigid' (double and semi-double) and 'De Caen' (single), can be grown as border plants, naturalized in grass, or simply grown for cutting. They surpass other types for brilliancy of colour and free-flowering habit.

HOW TO GROW

Grow the florist's anemones in damp, but not wet, humus-rich ground. Don't expect good results on poor soil.

Plant 5cm (2in) deep from early winter to mid spring, provided the ground is not too cold or frozen. In a sheltered position the tubers can be planted in mid autumn, about 8cm (3in) deep and 10–15cm (4–6in) apart. By staggering planting times, and using cloches or a cool or unheated greenhouse, the flowering season can be extended considerably.

The rock garden types, such as *A apennina, A. blanda* and *A. fulgens*, are planted in autumn, about 5cm (2in) deep and 10cm (4in) apart. This type of anemone takes time to become established, so plant

Anemone blanda

Anemone blanda 'Pink Star'

them in bold clumps of about a dozen tubers to try to achieve early impact. Once the clumps have established, they will spread and flower freely.

All the tuberous anemones will do best in a warm, sheltered spot, though many are very tough and hardy. To induce the tubers to sprout more readily, soak them in water for 48 hours before planting.

PROPAGATION

Old tubers can be divided, but it is better to plant young tubers from plants raised from seed. Sow as soon as the seeds are ripe, in

warmth or in a sheltered place outdoors.
The seeds have a downy covering, which tend
to make them cling together, so you may
have to rub them in dry sand first to separate
the seeds.

Be prepared to grow the seedlings on in a
nursery bed for a season or two before
planting in the final flowering positions.

POPULAR SPECIES

A. apennina (S. Europe and England). Clear
blue flowers, in mid spring. There is also a
white form. 10cm (4in).
A. blanda (S.E. Europe, Turkey). Blue,
white, red or pink daisy-like flowers, in late
winter or early or mid spring. 10cm (4in).
A. coronaria (S. Europe, Turkey). These
florist's anemones are represented by the

▲ *Anemone × fulgens* 'Annulata Grandiflora'

▼ *Anemone nemorosa*

Anemone coronaria 'De Caen' ▷

highly bred forms such as the single 'De Caen' group and the double and semi-double 'St. Brigid' group. 'St. Piran' is an improved De Caen type. The main flowering time is late spring and early summer. 23–30cm (9–12in) high.

A. nemorosa (Europe). Known as the wood anemone. Single, white, daisy-shaped flowers, in late spring. There are also double and lavender-blue forms. Makes good ground cover beneath trees or in front of shrubs. 15cm (6in).

A. pavonina (*A. fulgens*) (C. and E. Mediterranean). Scarlet flowers, with a black eye, in early and mid spring. One form

Anemone pavonina

Arisaema candidissimum

with large showy scarlet flowers with a pale yellow centre may be sold as *A. × Culgens annulata grandiflora*. 15–20cm (6–8in).

ARISAEMA

he name comes from the Greek *aron* (arum) and *haema* (blood), indicating their relationship to the arums.

You won't find these plants in many garden centres or even bulb catalogues, but they are worth searching out if you want something a little curious for the woodland garden. The arisaemas have hooded flower-like spathes and a tuberous root.

HOW TO GROW
Plant the tubers about 15cm (6in) deep in mid autumn, in a shady position. Add plenty of leaf-mould or peat.

PROPAGATION
Lift in early or mid spring, and remove offsets to replant.

POPULAR SPECIES
A. candidissimum (China). White spathe, sometimes pink-tinged, veined green, in early summer. 15cm (6in).

Arum creticum (see overleaf)

ARUM

Many arums are grown primarily for their distinctive spathes, though many also have attractive foliage, and some have distinctive spikes of bright red berries in the autumn.

You will probably have to go to a specialist for these plants, though you will also find them sold by some herbaceous plant nurseries.

HOW TO GROW

Grow in a moist position in partial shade. Plant to a depth of 10–15cm (4–6in) in late summer or early autumn where they can be left undisturbed.

PROPAGATION

Lift and remove offsets to replant when dormant.

POPULAR SPECIES

A. creticum (Crete, S. Greece). Pale yellow spathes in late spring. This species requires well-drained soil and a sunny position in order to flourish. 30cm (1ft).

A. italicum 'Pictum' (England to S.E. Europe, to Canary Is.). The large wavy leaves, marbled white, are produced in autumn. Pale yellow spathes appear in late spring and early summer; bright orange-red berries in autumn. 30cm (1ft).

Arum italicum 'Pictum'

B

BABIANA
(Baboon root)

The Latin name comes from the Afrikaans word *bobbejaan*, meaning baboon. Baboons dig up the corms for food, hence the common name.

These unusual members of the iris family have strongly pleated leaves and tubular-to funnel-shaped flowers, not unlike freesias. They may simply be sold as hybrids, and the colours range from blue to rose and rich crimson.

Although there are more than 50 species, very few are sold commercially, and even then they are not widely available.

Babiana, selection

Most are dwarf plants suitable for growing in pots, in the rock garden, or at the front of borders.

HOW TO GROW

Plant the corms about 15cm (6in) apart and cover with about 2.5cm (1in) of soil, in a position where they will receive sun for at least half the day. They need a well-drained soil, and should be lifted for the winter. Cut off the leaves after they have turned brown.

Babianas also make useful greenhouse pot-plants. Pot them in late autumn, about seven or eight corms to a 15cm (6in) pot, with about 2.5cm (1in) of compost over the top. Keep barely moist until the plants are about 2.5cm (1in) high, then water freely. Feed once the flower spikes are visible. Reduce watering after flowering and dry off once the leaves have turned yellow.

Store the bulbs in a dry, frost-free place; those in pots can be stored in the pots until it is time to start watering to start them into growth again.

PROPAGATION

Divide the corms after two or three years – they multiply rapidly and will need to be separated by then anyway.

POPULAR SPECIES

Garden hybrids. The corms usually sold by bulb merchants are hybrids derived from several South African species. 15–30cm (6–12in) high.

BEGONIA

The plants take their name from Michel Begon (1638–1710), a French patron of botany and for a time Governor of French Canada.

Begonias form a huge genus with perhaps 1,000 species, apart from the many hybrids that we grow. Many of them have fibrous roots, and just a few of the tuberous types are included here.

All the begonias described below make excellent greenhouse plants, a few make good houseplants, and some are useful bedding and container plants outdoors for the summer months. Most have a long flowering season, from early summer to autumn, and some of the indoor pot plant

Begonia rex

Begonia, 'Non-stop' pink shades

Begonia × tuberhybrida 'Pendula'

types of begonias can flower at almost any
month of the year.

The begonias that you buy from bulb
merchants are the *B. × tuberhybrida*
tuberous-rooted begonias. Some of these
have huge flowers as much as 15cm (6in)
across, though many of the cascading types
have much smaller flowers.

Cascade-type begonias are usually grown
in hanging baskets, though they are also
effective trailing over the edge of a
windowbox.

Pendulous begonias, usually listed as *B.
pendula*, are graceful plants with a trailing
habit. The flowers are usually semi-double,
although some are single, and smaller than

Begonia × *tuberhybrida* 'Camellia-flowered'

some of the more upright begonias.

'Non-stop' begonias are a fairly new group, easily raised from seed. They are a cross between the multiflora and double camellia-flowered types. They come into flower early, remain compact, and have good-sized flowers carried well above the foliage. They also flower prolifically for a long period.

HOW TO GROW

Begonias prefer a well-drained soil that contains plenty of humus. Indoors, the large-flowered and cascade types are seldom very successful, but the 'Rieger' type of begonias are extremely pretty and successful houseplants, given a little care.

The 'Elatior' hybrids, which include the 'Rieger' strains, should be watered freely when in flower, but be careful not to waterlog the compost. They like a reasonably humid atmosphere, but, as with all begonias, try not to wet the leaves, as this may encourage mildew. Feed once the plant is showing flower buds. The plants can be kept growing after flowering, but it is generally best to take cuttings (either tuber or leaf cuttings) and to discard the old plants.

Grow the rhizomatous begonias, such as the popular *B. rex* hybrids, in good light without direct sunshine, and make sure the compost never dries out during the growing season; keep the soil on the dry side during the winter if the temperature is cool. Maintain a humid atmosphere without wetting the leaves. Repot each spring, using a peat-based compost.

Grow tuberous begonias in pots in a greenhouse, or in containers or open ground outdoors once danger of frost has passed. They do best in cool summer weather in good light (but not necessarily direct full sun), but without too much wind or rain. If the weather becomes too hot, however, buds may drop.

Start the tubers off in pots or trays of compost a couple of months before planting out time (which should be after the danger of frost), using a peaty compost. If you are not sure which way up to plant the tubers, the rounded side is the bottom and the side with the depression is the top. Bury tubers

Rieger *Begonia*

Rieger *Begonia*

almost to the rim, but do not let soil collect in the saucer-shaped depression on the top.

Once shoots have appeared and the tubers have rooted, transfer to pots or containers, or plant outdoors. Be prepared to feed the plants in early and mid summer, but stop feeding in late summer.

In autumn the leaves will begin to turn yellow, and the plants must be lifted before the frosts arrive. If necessary, leave them in boxes to become dormant. Remove the remains of the old stems before storing in a frost-free place.

If the large-flowered tuberous begonias are being grown as pot plants, remove the small winged female flowers that form either side of the central male flowers (the big ones that you want to encourage).

PROPAGATION

Most of the begonias mentioned here are easily propagated from tuber cuttings taken in spring. Cut off the new shoots when they are 2.5cm (1in) or so high, and root these. Old tubers can be divided so that each piece has shoots, but this is not such a satisfactory method of propogation.

B. rex is also easy to root from leaf cuttings. Lay a mature but not old leaf flat on the surface of cuttings compost, slit through the main veins with a sharp knife or razor-blade, and use pegs of weights (such as small stones) to keep the leaf in contact with the compost. If kept moist and humid new plants should soon form where the leaf has been cut.

B. rex and the 'Non-stop' begonias can also be raised from seed very successfully, although the seed is very fine and needs generous warmth for quick germination.

POPULAR SPECIES

'Hiemalis' and 'Rieger' types (hybrids derived from B. socotrana). Small single or double flowers in shades of red, orange, and yellow. Some have dark-coloured foliage. 23–30cm (9–12in).

B. rex (Assam). It is the hybrids with beautifully marked and brilliantly coloured leaves that are grown. 30cm (1ft).

B. × tuberhybrida (garden origin). Large double male flowers (the smaller female flowers are best removed, if pot grown) can be 15cm (6in) across. Early summer to early autumn. There are many named varieties, but the tubers are often sold just by colours, which include reds, pinks, oranges, yellows, and white. 30–45cm (1–1½ft).

BLETILLA

The Latin diminutive of *Bletia* is *Bletilla*, a genus in which some species were formerly placed.

Just one species of this small genus of terrestrial orchids is likely to be offered for sale: *B. striata*. Although it can be grown outdoors in mild, sheltered areas, at least for the summer, it is best grown in pots indoors or in a greenhouse. Being a small plant it needs to be seen at close range to be appreciated, which is another reason for growing it in pots.

HOW TO GROW

If growing outdoors, plant in well-drained soil enriched with leaf-mould or peat, and protect with a mulch of bracken, coarse sand, or pulverized bark for the winter. Although it will tolerate a sunny position, it prefers a sheltered, semi-shady spot.

Grow indoors in 15cm (6in) pots, in a fibrous compost (equal parts peat, loam, leaf-mould, sphagnum moss and coarse sand is a good mixture, but a peat-based compost will do). Cover the rhizomes with about 2.5cm (1in) of compost or soil. Water the compost freely during the growing period, but only just enough to keep it slightly damp during the dormant period. Feed with a liquid fertilizer during the summer.

Maintain a winter temperature of 5°C (41°F), but ventilate freely whenever the temperature is over 13°C (55°F). Repot in spring, every second year.

PROPAGATION

Divide in early or mid spring, replanting the pseudobulbs.

POPULAR SPECIES

B. striata (*Bletia hyacinthina*) (China and Japan). Tufts of slender, grassy leaves, and small sprays of mauve-pink flowers resembling tiny cattleya orchids with purple lips, in late spring or early summer. There is also a white form. 23–30cm (9–12in).

Bletilla striata

BRODIAEA

The brodiaeas are rather lanky plants, which need to be massed in a group to be seen at their best, perhaps in a 'wild' area of the garden. They are also worth growing as a cut flower. Once established they multiply freely and should form a trouble-free clump that will need little attention.

Brodiaea laxa

HOW TO GROW

Plant the corms in autumn 10cm (4in) deep, in groups of five or six, in a well-drained soil. Choose a sunny sheltered position.

PROPAGATION

Lift an established clump, remove the small corms and grow them on. It may be necessary to grow small corms on for a couple of years before they become established and reach flowering size.

They can be raised from seed, sown in warmth in a greenhouse, but will take three to five years to flower.

POPULAR SPECIES

B. laxa (*Triteleia laxa*) (California). Loose heads of blue tubular flowers in mid summer. 60cm (2ft).

BULBOCODIUM

The name comes from the Greek *bolbos* (bulb) and *kodion* (wool), alluding to the layer of hairs between the corm and its skin or tunic.

There is just one species in this genus – *B. vernum*. It is not widely available, but can be obtained from specialist bulb merchants. It is worth searching out, as a group of bulbocodiums makes a refreshing sight as you come across them on a cold spring morning. It is among the earliest bulbs to flower, and looks good in a rock garden or raised bed. It also makes a pretty pot-plant for a cold greenhouse. The purple flowers, which appear in February or March, look rather like lavender-pink crocuses. They appear before the leaves, or at least while the foliage is still small. The flowers appear

Bulbocodium vernum

over a period of two to three weeks.

This is a tough plant, and does well even in very cold areas.

HOW TO GROW

Grow in a well-drained, sunny site. Plant the corms about 10cm (4in) apart in the early autumn, covering them with a layer of about 8cm (3in) of soil.

PROPAGATION

Lift established clumps when the leaves are dying down, separate and replant every third or fourth year.

POPULAR SPECIES

B. vernum (Europe). Lavender-pink, tubular, crocus-like flowers, more star-like when fully open, which bloom in late winter and early spring. The species has tufts of strap-like foliage. 10cm (4in).

C

CALADIUM
(Angel's wing)

aladiums are magnificent foliage plants. The large, shield-shaped but very thin leaves that give the plant its common name, come in various combinations, usually with shades of green, white, red, and pink. Some have contrasting margins, or veins, others are more mottled.

They would be much more popular if they were just that little bit easier to grow. In some warm, humid parts of the United States they are grown outdoors during the summer, but in less favourable places, and certainly in Britain, they must be regarded as greenhouse plants or houseplants. Even indoors they are not easy, as they demand high humidity as well as warmth and good light.

Growing plants are sometimes available in garden centres, but don't expect to find the tubers in shops or garden centres. You will probably have to send away to a specialist in uncommon bulbs.

HOW TO GROW

Plant the tuber 2.5cm (1in) deep in early spring, and start it into growth at about 24°C (75°F), keeping the atmosphere humid; a propagator is probably the best place.

Grow on in a greenhouse or indoors. Avoid direct sun, but make sure there is plenty of bright, indirect light.

To keep this plant happy, maintain a humid atmosphere; if necessary, mist the leaves every day without making them too wet.

If flowers appear (they look like small calla lilies), remove them; you want the plant to put all its energy into producing foliage.

Water freely during the summer, and feed regularly from mid summer until the leaves begin to shrivel and fall in autumn. Once this happens, gradually withhold water until the tuber becomes dormant. Keep it in the pot for the winter, making sure the temperature does not fall too low, then repot and start the tuber into growth again in spring.

PROPAGATION

Divide the tubers once they have started into growth, provided each piece has an eye. Grow them on in a heated propagator initially.

POPULAR SPECIES

C. ×*hortulanum* (garden origin). These are hybrids derived from *C. bicolor* (which originates from the Amazon jungle), and there are several named varieties. 30cm (1ft) high.

CAMASSIA
(Quamash)

I t was the Northwest American Indians that gave this bulb the name of quamash, a word which was used for an edible species of the plant. The Americans often consider the quamash a counterpart to the British bluebell.

These plants thrive best in moist woodland conditions, but the dwarf kinds are more effective in groups in a border, planted beside a pool, or naturalized in grass in a wild garden.

HOW TO GROW

Plant the bulbs about 10cm (4in) deep in autumn, spacing them at least 15cm (6in) apart. If possible choose a moist position in heavy soil.

Water freely in the spring and in the early summer if the soil is dry, and dead-head after flowering.

PROPAGATION

Lift mature clumps of camassias in the early autumn, and remove the small bulbs to grow on until they are large enough to plant where they are to flower.

Sowing seed is a slow method, as the plants may take three to five years to flower, but useful if you need a lot of plants for naturalizing in grass. Sow fresh seed in pots in a cold frame in summer. Pot up the seedlings individually into 13cm (5in) pots when they are ready (which may take more than 12 months), and plunge the pots outdoors. Plant out when large enough.

Camassia cusickii

POPULAR SPECIES

C. cusickii (N.W. USA). This species has tall spikes of blue star-like flowers 4cm (1½in) wide on stiff upright stems; the leaves are greyish-green up to 35cm (1ft 2in). It blooms in early and mid summer. 60–90cm (2–3ft).
C. leichtlinii (Oregon). This species has spikes of dark blue, cream or white flowers, with conspicuous yellow anthers, 4–8cm (1½–3in) wide. 1m (3ft) high.
C. quamash (*C. esculenta*) (California, Canada). The bulbs of this species are edible. Spikes of blue, purple, or white flowers, approximately 4–8cm (1½–3in) in width, are carried well above the foliage in summer. 75cm (2½ft) high.

Camassia leichtlinii 'Flore Pleno'

CANNA
(Indian shot)

The name comes from the Greek word *kanna*, meaning reed, reflecting the tall, seed-like stems of some species.

Cannas are often seen in public gardens and parks, where they are frequently used to give summer bedding a tropical look, but they are too seldom grown in smaller gardens. They can grow tall and big but there is plenty of scope for using them around the garden besides making splendid accent plants among summer bedding. Try a whole narrow border of them, perhaps with a hedge as a background, or a group of them in a herbaceous border, or even in a large tub on the patio. Cannas also make excellent conservatory plants.

The long flowering period of the canna makes them an especially good buy. They start blooming once the really warm weather arrives, and continue until the chills of autumn. Many of them have the bonus of dark bronze or varigated foliage with a lushness that commands attention.

They are clump-forming plants with fleshy, tuber-like rhizomes, and in favourable areas are hardy enough to be left outdoors over the winter with suitable protection.

HOW TO GROW

Start the rhizomes into growth in early or mid spring (mid spring is early enough for plants that are to be bedded out), covering them thinly with moist peat, and maintaining a temperature of about 15°C (60°F). Pot up into 15cm (6in) pots of good compost; either grow on in a container, or plant out once danger of frost has passed. Space the plants 30cm (1ft) apart in beds or borders, covering the tubers with approximately 3cm (1in) of soil.

Water freely throughout the growing season; feeding should not be necessary unless the soil is impoverished.

After the first autumn frost kills the foliage, lift and store the rhizomes in a

Canna 'Lucifer'

frost-free place. If you leave them in the ground for the winter cover the area with 15cm (6in) of sand, pulverized bark, or bracken (which must be removed in late spring). If you can overwinter them outdoors, the plants will gradually spread to form bold clumps; but there's always the risk of losing them.

Cannas

PROPAGATION

Divide the rhizomes in spring. Start them off in warmth in a greenhouse or indoors in early or mid spring, and then divide them into portions each with a single shoot and roots when the leaves are about 7–10cm (3–4in) high.

Cannas can be raised from seed, but this needs care and patience. The seeds are very hard (they used to be used as a substitute for shot, hence their common name), and you should file the hard outer coat without damaging the actual seed. Then soak the seeds in tepid water (leave in the water for 24 hours) before sowing. Germinate at a temperature of 21–23°C (70–75°F). Germination may take up to a couple of months, or an even longer period of time, and is likely to be erratic.

POPULAR SPECIES

The hybrids, derived from such species as *C. flaccida. C. coccinea*, and *C. indica*. They include 'Lucifer' (scarlet, edged with yellow; green foliage), 'Dazzler' (red; bronze-purple foliage), 'President' (vivid scarlet), and 'Coq d'Or'. There are dwarfs of less than 60cm (2ft), and tall ones that can reach 1.8m (6ft), but most of the hybrids grow to about 1–1.2m (3–4ft) high.

Canna hybrid

Canna 'Coq d'Or'   *Canna* 'President'

Cardiocrinum giganteum

CARDIOCRINUM
(Giant Lily)

The name is derived from two Greek words: *kardia* (heart) and *krinon* (lily), alluding to the heart-shaped leaves and lily-like flowers.

Big, bold plants (especially *C. giganteum*), the cardiocrinums are useful for sheltered mixed borders of the edge of woodland.

HOW TO GROW

Cardiocrinums prefer a sheltered position in partial shade, and a moist, humus–rich soil.

Plant the bulbs 90cm (3ft) apart in autumn, with the nose just covered with soil.

The original bulb dies after flowering, and leaves behind small offset bulbs; these can take three or four years to reach flowering size, so it's a good idea to plant a group of bulbs of different sizes, to ensure continuity of flowering over the next few years.

The young shoots of *C. cordatum* emerge early and may need protection, therefore, from late frosts.

Mulch with well-rotted manure or garden compost each spring, and water freely in dry weather during the growing season.

PROPAGATION

Leave the offsets to increase the size of the clump or remove and grow them on elsewhere.

Seed, sown when it is ripe (or in spring), is a slow option. The seedlings are likely to take six years or even longer to reach flowering size.

POPULAR SPECIES

C. cordatum (Japan). The main basal leaves are arranged on a rosette, with the leafy flowering spike appearing in late summer. The big, creamy-white, bell-like flowers, streaked with yellow and marked purple inside, are up to 15cm (6in) long. 1.2–1.8m (4–6ft) high.

C. giganteum (Himalaya). Similar to *C. cordatum*, but hardier and larger, with the leaves arranged in a spiral up the stem. The hanging flowers, like white bells at the top of the spike, are sometimes 15cm (6in) long, and appear in mid and late summer. 1.8–3m (6–10ft).

CHIONODOXA
(Glory of the snow)

Although some of the chionodoxas flower in late winter, when the snow is still around, it is early or mid spring before most come into their glory. In their native habitat,

Chionodoxa luciliae

Chionodoxa gigantea

however, they do flower as the snow melts.

Planted in a mass, especially in bold drifts or naturalized in grass, they are surprisingly colourful and attractive.

HOW TO GROW

Plant the bulbs about 3–8cm (1–3in) apart in well-drained soil in the autumn. Cover with about 5cm (2in) of soil. They do best in full sun but will still put on a good performance in light shade.

Leave undisturbed in the ground to multiply and naturalize.

PROPAGATION

Lift established groups and replant the offset bulbs after flowering. Large bulbs can be replanted to flower the next season, small ones may have to be grown on for a season or two.

Seed is another alternative, and some self-sown seedlings are likely to appear in the garden anyway. Collect the seed pods before the seeds scatter, and sow the seeds when they are ripe, in a cold frame or in a spare piece of ground. Grow them on in a nursery bed, and plant in their flowering positions during the second summer.

POPULAR SPECIES

C. gigantea (*C. grandiflora*) (Asia Minor). The species with the largest flowers; the

Chionodoxa luciliae among heathers

Chionodoxa sardensis

Chlidanthus fragrans

lilac-blue starry flowers with a white eye are about 2.5cm (1in) wide. Early to mid spring. 15cm (6in).

C. luciliae (Asia Minor). Loose sprays of deep blue flowers with a white centre, early spring. One of the best for naturalizing. There is also a pink form. 15cm (6in).

C. sardensis (Asia Minor). Gentian blue flowers with a small white eye, early to late spring. 15cm (6in).

CHLIDANTHUS

The name comes from the Greek *chlide* (luxury) and *anthos* (a flower). It shouldn't be regarded as a luxury, however, as the bulbs are not very expensive. Even so, don't expect to find this unusual bulb in garden centres, or even in many of the popular bulb catalogues. It is available, however, from specialist bulb suppliers, and it is worth seeking out if you want something a little different.

It is a summer-flowering bulb that can be attractive in a pot, and even makes an excellent cut flower. The yellow tubular flowers, spreading into broad petals at the end, are pleasantly fragrant and smell like some of the lilies; in some countries the plant is called the perfumed fairy lily.

HOW TO GROW

Plant in well-drained soil in full sun, in spring. If planting outdoors, space about 15cm (6in) apart, preferably in a raised bed so that you can appreciate them more easily, covered with 3–5cm (1–2in) of soil. It is a good idea to plant three bulbs to a 15cm (6in) pot, which can be plunged outdoors for the summer and taken into a greenhouse for the winter.

Water freely during the growing season, and apply a general balanced fertilizer once flowering is over.

Lift the bulbs (or if growing in plunged pots, take the pots indoors) in autumn. The dormant bulbs can be overwintered in their pots, or if simply lifted from the ground, stored in dry peat or vermiculite once they have dried off.

PROPAGATION

Separate the small bulbs that form at the base of the old ones before the leaves die down in autumn.

POPULAR SPECIES

C. fragrans (Peru). Small, yellow, lily-like flowers on sprays among narrow, grassy foliage, in mid summer. 25cm (10in).

COLCHICUM
(Meadow saffron, autumn crocus)

These bright sparks of autumn derive their Latin name from Colchis, at the eastern end of the Black Sea, where they were said to grow. They should not be confused with the true crocuses (of which there are autumn-flowering species). The colchicums have much larger flowers, ranging in colour from red-purple, lilac, pink and white, which appear before the leaves (another common name is naked ladies).

For a bit of fun, try a couple of the corms on a window-sill (placing them on a saucer of sand will help to keep them more stable), then watch the flowers appear even though the bulb is not planted. Don't try to do this two years running. As soon as a corm has produced its indoor fun show, plant it in the garden. The large leaves will appear in spring, and you should be able to look

Colchicum agrippinum

forward to a repeat performance in the garden each autumn for many years.

The colchicums flower when most of the other plants in the garden are beginning to show signs of coming to an end for the season, so try to find room for plenty of them. Rock gardens are an obvious home for them, but they are also useful at the front of borders, and can be very effective, too, in gravel gardens.

The only problem with colchicums is that the leaves that appear in spring are rather large and ungainly, so in a border it's a good idea to plant them along with herbaceous plants which grow up and take over in spring, dying down in time for the colchicums to come into stage in the autumn. Try using these bulbs beneath trees (provided the shade is not too dense).

HOW TO GROW

Plant the corms in late summer or early autumn. They will be happy in full sun or partial shade, and respond to a rich soil.

Plant about 20cm (8in) apart, and cover the corms with about 10cm (4in) of soil. Leave them undisturbed to form established clumps.

PROPAGATION

Lift or divide an established group and replant the offset corms. The best time to do this is after the leaves have died down, usually in early or mid summer. Grow small corms on in a nursery bed for a year or two – they should flower successfully after three

Colchicum speciosum

Colchicum speciosum 'Album'

or four years.

Growing them from seed is slow, but useful if you require a large number of plants. Sow in pots in a cold frame in early or mid summer, and leave the seedlings (which can take 18 months to germinate) in the pots to grow on for about a year. Then plant out into a nursery bed until ready for planting in the flowering positions. It may take the plants anything from four to six years to reach flowering size.

POPULAR SPECIES

C. agrippinum (origin uncertain). Mottled flowers – red-purple on a white background; in early autumn. 10–15cm (4–6in).
C. autumnale (Europe). Lilac, pink, or white flowers, early or mid autumn. There

are double forms. 15cm (6in) high.
C. byzantinum (Asia Minor). This species has large lilac-pink flowers, which appear early in the autumn. The broad leaves, which appear in spring, can double the flowering height of 15cm (6in).
C. cilicicum (Turkey). Pink to yellow flowers in mid autumn. 23cm (9in).
C. speciosum (Persia, Caucasus, Asia Minor, Syria, Lebanon). This species has large, goblet-shaped, light to bright rosy-red flowers in early and mid autumn. There is also a white form. In spring the leaves double the flowering height of 15cm (6in). There are several widely available hybrids, such as 'Violet Queen' (violet), and 'Water Lily' (large, double lilac-pink flowers that spread wide in the sun).

Colchicum 'Autumn Queen'

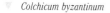 *Colchicum autumnale*

▼ *Colchicum byzantinum*   ▼ *Colchicum cilicicum*

Corydalis solida

CORYDALIS

These plants all have small flowers resembling a snapdragon (the name of the genus is from a Greek word meaning 'crested lark', the spurs of the flowers being likened to those of the bird). They are carried on short stems, usually nestling among the fern-like foliage.

They are not showy plants, but worth considering for naturalizing in a cold, moist position. Some, such as *C. solida* (probably the most widely available of the species mentioned here), make pretty pot plants for an alpine house or to grow in a cold frame to take indoors just for the flowering period.

The species listed below form tubers, but some of the other species have fibrous roots. Even the tuberous ones are unlikely to be stocked by garden centres; be prepared to go to a specialist in the less common bulbs to find them.

HOW TO GROW

Plant to a depth of 5cm (2in) in autumn in a well-drained but moisture-retentive soil. They will grow in sun but generally have more luxurious growth in partial shade. Leave the plants undisturbed to become established.

PROPAGATION

Divide established clumps. Seed is another option if you need a large number of plants.

POPULAR SPECIES

C. ambigua (Japan). Clear blue flowers (sometimes violet) over attractively divided foliage in mid spring. 15cm (6in).
C. bracteate (Siberia). A very hardy species with clear yellow flowers in late spring and early summer. 20cm (8in).
C. solida (Europe). Perhaps the most likely available of the species listed here, and easy to grow. Pink-purple flowers in mid spring. 15cm (6in).

CRINUM
(Cape lily)

There are almost 100 species of crinum (the name is based on the Greek word *krinon*, a lily). These plants are true bulbs. The flowers, like the bulbs, are large and produced like ordinary lilies on tall stems. Some are star shaped; all have a very strong and sweet fragrance. The colours are rose, pink and white.

Originally, crinums come from mainly tropical and sub-tropical countries and only a few are hardy enough to grow outdoors, in sunny and sheltered spots. They like narrow, warm, flower borders, preferably backed by a warm wall. Grow them through dwarf shrubs for a striking effect; or for safety, plant them in large tubs which you can move indoors when the weather gets chilly. In very cold areas, even the hardiest types should be grown in a frost-free greenhouse.

The plants are deep-rooted, dislike being disturbed, but multiply rapidly. They usually flower in late summer or autumn although *C. asiaticum* will flower on and off all summer if the weather is warm enough.

HOW TO GROW

The soil should be deep and fertile, but well drained – any commercial, preferably loam-based, potting mixture is suitable. Choose a suitably warm place, and cover the bulbs with at least 15cm (6in) of soil. In pots, where space is more limited, plant them with the necks either at or just beneath the

Crinum × powellii

Crinum moorei

surface of the soil.

Emerging shoots should be protected from frost with coarse sand, dry peat or some similar form of insulation. Water regularly and generously in summer and apply liquid fertilizer at fortnightly intervals, once the foliage is growing well. In very hot areas, some shade may be needed.

PROPAGATION

Propagation from seed is slow; it is better to use offsets, removed carefully from mature bulbs. Lift the bulbs in early spring, not more than once every three or four years, and replant immediately.

POPULAR SPECIES

C. bulbispermum (*C. longifolium*) (South Africa). Wide open, white flowers,

sometimes flushed with pink, produced in early and mid autumn. 45cm (1½ft).
C. moorei (South Africa). Spreading evergreen leaves, and large white and pink flowers from mid summer to early autumn. 60cm (2ft).
C. × powellii (garden origin). Flowers vary in shade from pink to white. Large and lily-like, they open in succession from mid summer to early autumn. 90cm (3ft).

CROCOSMIA

The dried flowers of crocosmia smell of saffron, hence the name, from the Greek words *krokos* (saffron) and *osme* (smell). The leaves are flat and sword-like, the flowers yellow, orange or red, borne in arching spikes from mid summer to the early autumn.

Crocosmias add a touch of life to any herbaceous border, and make very good cut flowers, lasting about a fortnight in water. They are more often sold as growing plants than as dried corms, though they are available from specialist bulb suppliers, and sometimes in garden centres.

HOW TO GROW

Plant crocosmias 7–10cm (3–4in) deep, in clumps. They like a sunny, open situation, and well-drained sandy soil, enriched with compost or well-rotted manure. Keep them well watered in summer.

The best time for planting is early autumn, but spring is also satisfactory. Apply a light fertilizer when the shoots first appear. Remove the stems after all the flowers have died (unless you want to save the seeds for propagation).

Lift a few corms in autumn, to be replanted the following spring. Clean them and store in a frost-free and fairly dry place. Don't let the corms dry out completely, however, as they may shrivel up and die.

PROPAGATION

Propagate either by division or from seed. Sow the seeds as soon as they are ripe, several to a 13cm (5in) pot, in a cool greenhouse or frame. Let them grow undisturbed until the following mid summer (they will probably germinate in spring), then uncover them and harden off. They should flower one or two years later.

Lift and divide the clumps every three or four years, just after flowering time or before growth starts in early spring.

POPULAR SPECIES

C. × crocosmiiflora (*Montbretia crocosmiiflora*) (garden origin). A cross between the colourful *C. aurea* and the

Crocosmia masonorum

Crocosmia × crocosmiiflora 'Citronella'

hardy, vigorous *C. pottsii*. Yellow, orange and red flowers, small and star-shaped, produced in sprays on wiry stems, from mid summer to early autumn. Popular varieties include 'Solfataire' (apricot yellow with bronze-green leaves), and 'Vulcan' (orange red) 60–90cm (2–3ft).

C. masonorum (South Africa). Bold, beautiful plants, larger and more robust than most other crocosmias, as well as more hardy. Long, closely packed, arching sprays of brilliant orange-scarlet flowers bloom in mid summer. The leaves are strap-like and ribbed. 60cm (2ft).

CROCUS

These delicate-looking small plants are in fact remarkably hardy. They are cormous and originate from the Mediterranean and parts of Europe. The genus contains more than 70 species and countless varieties.

Small-flowered species crocuses are the earliest to flower, but the large-flowered hybrids, sometimes called Dutch hybrids, are more popular and well known, being more showy.

Most people associate crocuses with early and mid spring, but there are a number of autumn-flowering species, notably the famous saffron crocus.

Crocuses are ideal for containers of all kinds – pots, tubs and windowboxes. They can even be grown indoors. They look marvellous planted in drifts, or for spot colour on rock gardens and between stepping stones. The large-flowered types are excellent for naturalizing in grass, ideally beneath deciduous trees which don't cast too much shade, such as silver birch. After flowering, they won't look unsightly – the leaves, being small and narrow, blend in with the grass – and they will multiply freely if left to their own devices, which is when they are seen at their best. Species that flower in autumn, before the leaves appear, can be effectively combined with all kinds of ground-cover plants.

Crocuses are very sensitive to weather, closing when it is cloudy or stormy and opening in warm sunlight (except for *C.*

▲ *Crocus tomasinianus*

sativus). Grown indoors in the warmth, they will stay open for much longer.

HOW TO GROW

Crocuses need not be planted very deeply and, having contractile roots, they will adjust themselves if you get the depth wrong. Bury them about 2.5cm (1in) below the surface, at a distance roughly equal to the bulb depth. They will grow in almost any type of soil, but it must be well drained or the bulbs may rot. They need plenty of sun, and object to prolonged periods of wet weather. After flowering the leaves get much longer, and seed capsules appear before they die away.

Plant late winter- and spring-flowering crocuses in autumn, and autumn-flowering types in summer. If growing for the cold greenhouse (for which crocuses are excellent), plant in pans of a loam-based potting mixture.

Water regularly but not too heavily from the time the leaves first appear until they start dying. Don't remove the flowers or leaves before they are quite dead. When the leaves are yellow, they can be pulled off.

PROPAGATION

Sow seed, gathered when it ripens in the seed capsules. Seeds from garden hybrids will give varied results; it is safer to collect from species if you want a particular type of

crocus. Gather the seed capsules as soon as they begin to split open, and sow the seeds in pots or boxes of seed compost, covered over to a depth of about 1cm (½in). The seedlings must be grown on for two years before being planted out.

Alternatively, divide and replant offsets. After the leaves have turned brown and the plant is dormant, dig it up and carefully detach the cormlets. Dry them in shallow trays in the warmth. Remove dead leaves, skin and roots (but not the outer coat, or tunic). Large cormlets can be replanted in the soil, and should flower the following year. Small ones can also be replanted, but will take about two years to reach flowering

size. Keep them in a separate bed, if you have the space.

POPULAR SPECIES

C. ancyrensis (Turkey). Relatively long-lasting yellow flowers in late winter and early spring, free flowering. 5–8cm (2–3in).

C. angustifolius (*C. susianus*) (Russia). Spring-flowering. Massed close together, these crocuses look like a gold cloak spread over the ground, hence their common name 'cloth of gold'. Deep-orange flowers, feathered with mahogany on the outside, star-shaped and medium-sized. 6–7.5cm (2½–3in).

C. asturicus (Spain). High, pointed, mauve flowers, in early and mid autumn. *C. a.* 'Atropurpureus' is a deeper purple. The leaves develop after the flowers are over.

C. aureus (*C. luteus*) (Turkey). This is a robust species, good for planting in short grass. The leaves are broad and a glossy deep green. The flowers are neat and cup-shaped, deep yellow or orange, sometimes feathered bronze, and appear in mid spring. 'Dutch yellow' is a very popular and hardy hybrid of this species. *C. a. lacteus* is milky white. 8cm (3in).

C. banaticus (*C. iridiflorus*, *C. byzantinus*) (Hungary and Romania). The leaves appear in spring, after the flowers, which bloom in autumn. The flowers are 8–10cm (3–4in) high, with three tall outer petals, clear purple, and three inner petals, much smaller and paler in colour. The outer petals often reflex back, in the way that irises do. 10cm (4in) high.

C. biflorus (Italy and Asia Minor). Commonly known as the Scotch Crocus, this flowers in early spring. The flowers are quite large 10cm (4in), lilac-purple on the outside and white inside. There are forms that are lilac inside with darker veining outside, some with bold stripes and a yellow throat, and a pure white. 10cm (4in).

C. chrysanthus (Greece and Turkey). A very popular species, with many varieties and hybrids. The flowers are golden-yellow and bloom in early spring. The leaves are short and narrow and appear simultaneously with the flowers. Some of the most commonly grown hybrids are the free-flowering

▲ *Crocus ancyrensis* 'Golden Bunch'

▲ *Crocus chrysanthus* 'Cream Beauty'

▼ *Crocus biflorus weldenii*

▼ *Crocus laevigatus*

'Bluebird' (pure white inside with a violet-blue exterior); 'Blue Pearl' (a soft and delicate blue, silvery blue inside, with a bronze base); 'Princess Beatrix' (clear blue with darker blue feathering towards the golden-yellow base); and 'Zwanenburg Bronze' (golden-yellow inside with a dark bronze exterior). 8cm (3in).

C. goulimyi (S. Greece). The attractive lavender flowers bloom in autumn. The narrow leaves appear just before or just after the flowers. 10cm (4in).

C. imperati (S. Italy). Flowers in late winter and early spring. It will multiply rapidly during the summer, in dry spots. The flowers are mauve or purple centred with yellow, cup-shaped, and produced on quite long stalks. 10cm (4in).

C. kotschyanus (*C. zonatus*) (Lebanon). Flowers in early or mid autumn. The blooms are lilac-blue, throated with orange-yellow. The leaves appear after the flowers. 10cm (4in) high.

C. laevigatus (Greece). Fragrant pale lavender to white flowers, vivid purple, from mid autumn to early winter. 8cm (3in).

C. longiflorus (*C. odorus*) (Italy). Flowers in mid or late autumn, and is hardy to cold,

 Crocus sativus

 Crocus 'Vanguard'

 *Crocus speciosus* 'Oxonian'

Crocus vernus vernus

despite its origins. The flowers are large and globular, purple-lilac on the outside, blue-purple inside, with orange throats, and a strong scent. 8–10cm (3–4in).

C. sativus (Italy and Turkey). This is the saffron crocus. The flowers are quite large and a rich purple-red, with large red stigmas and orange anthers; they bloom in autumn. They remain open even in cloudy weather, unlike other crocuses. Unfortunately *C. sativus* is not very easy to grow in cool areas because it needs long periods of sustained warmth. 10cm (4in).

C. sieberi (Crete and the Greek mainland).

One of the best and most vigorous of the spring-flowering species. The original species is mauve with an orange-yellow throat and rich red stigmas. There is also a white form. 8–10cm (3–4in).

C. speciosus (E. Europe and Asia Minor). Very easy to grow, this showy crocus has unusually large, bright lilac flowers, with yellow anthers and scarlet stigmas, which appear from early to mid autumn. There are many useful garden hybrids, such as pure white 'Albus', 'Artabir' (pale blue streaked with dark blue) and 'Oxonian', a distinctive dark violet-blue. 13cm (5in).

Crocuses Dutch hybrids

Crocus 'Pickwick'

Crocus 'Joan of Arc'

C. tomasinianus (Dalmatia). The buds appear in late winter, the flowers in early spring with lilac inner petals and a pale mauve exterior. Some varieties are a deeper mauve or purple. 8–10cm (3–4in).
C. vernus (Alps and Pyrenees). Flowers in spring. The species itself is seldom grown, but is a parent of many of the very popular and showy Dutch hybrids.
Dutch hybrids These are the large-flowered spring crocuses so widely planted for easy spring colour. Good ones include 'Joan of Arc' (white), 'Little Dorrit' (silvery-lilac), 'Queen of the Blues' (lavender-blue), and the large 'Purpureus Grandiflorus' (purple), but there are several other fine varieties.

CYCLAMEN

The genus name is probably a contraction of the Greek word *kyklaminos*, from *kyklos*, a circle (possibly alluding to the coiled stem of the seed vessel).

The large-flowered tender cyclamens (derived from *C. persicum*) that are such popular pot plants during the winter moths, are known by almost everyone, whether they are gardeners or not. The hardy cyclamens are obscure by comparison, but they are widely available and well worth growing.

Grow florist's cyclamen indoors or in a greenhouse. Hardy cyclamens prefer filtered shade, and grow well beneath trees that do not have a very dense canopy (though they will even grow close to the trunk of beech and oak trees); they will also grow in leafy soil in front of shrubs.

Apart from size, the flowers of the tender and hardy species are very similar, but the plants need different treatment (see below). The florist's cyclamens are usually in flower, and on sale, from late autumn to late winter, though they can be bought at other times. The miniature hardy species generally flower in autumn or spring. The autumn-flowering species are especially useful because they bring a little late colour when most other plants have finished.

Many cyclamens have very attractively variegated foliage.

HOW TO GROW

The florist's cyclamens will grow in any good potting compost, and seem to do particularly well in loam-based composts. When the plants are in flower, grow them in an unheated room if you want the blooms to last, but the temperature should not fall below 7°C (45°F). Avoid dry air, and don't wet the tuber more than necessary. (Stand the pot in a shallow bowl of water for a short time to allow water to seep through the compost, then remove it.)

Remove flowers and leaves as they fade, twisting them off close to the corm. Keep the plants in a light position, and feed them while they are in flower. When flowering is over, put the plants in a cool greenhouse or leave them on a light window-sill. When they stop producing new leaves, gradually reduce the amount and frequency of the water given. By early summer the leaves will probably have withered and watering can be stopped altogether.

Leave the tubers in their pots until late summer, then knock them out of the compost and repot with the top of the tubers just showing. Start watering again, and keep the plants in a greenhouse or cold frame. Start feed once they are beginning to show flower buds, and take them indoors again when the flowers are starting to open.

Hardy cyclamens need the minimum of care once planted and established. They do best, however, in a humus-rich loam that is well drained.

Plant them in late summer or early autumn, setting them about 15cm (6in) apart (the tubers of some species become very large and need room to expand). Plant the tubers shallowly, flat side down, and barely cover those of *C. hederifolium* (*C. neapolitanum*). Be careful as you plant them not to damage any protruberances, as these produce the flowers.

Water in dry weather until the plants become established, and if possible mulch with leaf-mould annually after flowering.

Cyclamen coum

Cyclamen graecum

Cyclamen hederifolium

Cyclamen repandum

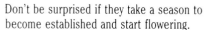

Don't be surprised if they take a season to become established and start flowering.

Sprinkle bonemeal or a general fertilizer over the area once a year, but don't fork or hoe it in as this may damage tubers near the surface (try hosing the bonemeal or fertilizer in if the weather is dry).

PROPAGATION

As cyclamen tubers do not divide satisfactorily, sowing seed is the method used for propagation. The florist's cyclamen is usually sown in gentle heat between late summer and early spring (consult seed catalogues for the best time to sow particular varieties – seed sown in late summer is likely to flower in early winter of the following year, but some modern varieties come into flower more quickly). Germination is likely to be slow and erratic (try soaking the seeds in water for 24 hours before sowing to help the process along).

Hardy cyclamens are usually sown in a cold frame or cool greenhouse between mid autumn and early spring. It can take the seedlings three to five years to reach flowering size.

POPULAR SPECIES

C. balearicum (Balearic Islands). Small, white or pink fragrant flowers in spring. Not hardy and best grown in pots in a cool greenhouse. 15cm (6in).
C. cilicicum (Asia Minor). Half-hardy; pale rose-pink flowers with darker blotch at base, in mid and late autumn. 10cm (4in).
C. coum (S.E. Europe, into Asia). A species with deep crimson, carmine, magenta, or white flowers from early winter to early spring. 8cm (3in).
C. europaeum (*C. purpurascens*) (Hungary to Italy). Hardy; deep carmine, fragrant flowers with deep blotch at base, mid summer to early autumn. There are paler forms, including a white form. 10cm (4in).
C. graecum (Greece). Best grown in pots in a greenhouse; red-pink to white flowers. Attractively variegated leaves. 10cm (4in).
C. hederifolium (*C. neapolitanum*) (S. Europe). Hardy; pink flowers with deeper blotch at base, in early and mid autumn. There is a white form. Attractively variegated leaves. 10cm (4in).
C. libanoticum (Lebanon). Best grown in pots in an alpine house in cold areas. The fragrant pink flowers, in late winter and early spring, are larger than on most miniature cyclamens. 15cm (6in).
C. persicum (E. Mediterranean). The species, a parent of the modern florist's cyclamen, is not normally grown. Consult seed catalogues for a range of up-to-date hybrids. There are miniature forms, and some are fragrant.
C. repandum (S. Europe). Pink, sometimes almost carmine flowers, from early to late spring. There is an uncommon white form. 15cm (6in) high.

D

DAHLIA

here are gardeners who regard dahlias as rather vulgar garden plants. It is another way of saying that they prefer plants closer to the wild species and that modern dahlias are highly bred – they come in all shapes, sizes and colours, and bear little resemblance to the species from which they were originally derived. The plants are named in honour of Dr Anders (Andreas?) Dahl (1751–89), a Swedish botanist.

It is always worth finding space for at least a few dahlias – either as cut flowers, or to provide late colour in a border, for massed bedding, or perhaps as an edging if you choose a dwarf variety, or even for the show bench.

Exhibitors almost always buy rooted cuttings from specialist nurseries (mainly because these have the best exhibition varieties and the latest novelties), but the tubers available from bulb merchants and garden centres are perfectly satisfactory.

If you want the best bedding dahlias, choose a good modern variety to grow from seed, or better still grow plants propagated from parents of proven merits.

Dahlia 'Carol' (Dwarf Bedding)

Dahlia 'Inca Breeder' (Medium Semi-cactus)

Dahlia 'Wootton Monarch' (Giant Semi-cactus)

Dahlia 'Pink Triumph' (Large Semi-cactus)

HOW TO GROW

Bedding dahlias do not need a very rich soil, but the larger kinds are gross feeders, and the ground needs thorough preparation if you want large blooms, or simply a profusion of flowers.

Incorporate as much well-rotted compost or manure as you can spare when digging over the ground before planting, and rake in a general balanced fertilizer.

Whether bought or raised from cuttings, plants must be hardened off thoroughly and planted out only after the likelihood of frost has passed, in late spring or early summer. Tubers can be planted in mid spring as it will take several weeks for the shoots to emerge. If frost is forecast after they have emerged, protect the shoots with a mulch or even newspaper and polythene.

Tubers can be started off indoors or in a greenhouse, in trays of moist peat or potting compost, and planted out in early summer. You can also use some of the shoots for cuttings. If planting tubers, dig holes large enough to take the tubers easily, setting them with the crown 5cm (2in) below the surface.

Tall types will need staking, and if using tubers insert the stake before returning the soil at planting time. Stakes inserted later may damage the tubers.

Water freely in dry weather to encourage large flowers. Regular feeding, especially with a liquid fertilizer, should bring good results – but don't use fertilizers with a very high nitrogen content otherwise there may be too much leaf growth at the expense of the flowers.

Exhibition types, or those grown for cut flowers where you want a long, clean stem, will require disbudding. Side buds usually grow out from the leaf axils behind the main crown buds, and removing these produces the desired long stems with large flowers. For even bigger blooms (and this is worthwhile only if you are growing the larger decorative kinds of dahlias), the number of shoots can be thinned too.

Flowering will gradually deteriorate towards the end of the season, and the first

Dahlia 'Tahiti Sunrise' (Medium Semi-cactus)

Dahlia 'Hamari Gold' (Giant Decorative)

Dahlia 'Hamari Bride' (Medium Cactus)

Dahlia 'Highgate Torch' (Medium Semi-cactus)

Dahlia 'Doris Day' (Small Cactus)

frost will blacken the foliage. As soon as possible afterwards, lift the plants and leave them in a dry frost-proof place, such as the greenhouse or a shed, to allow the soil to dry off the tubers.

When the tubers have dried, cut the old stem back to within an inch or so of the crown, then stand them upside down so that any moisture in the hollow stems will drain out. Store in a dry, frost-proof place, but avoid a warm position where they will dry out too much. Store them in dry peat, or vermiculite. Dust them with a fungicide before storing to ensure that they overwinter without rotting, but also check the tubers once or twice during the winter months and remove any that look unhealthy.

PROPAGATION

Bedding dahlias are very easy to raise from seed, sown in warmth in late winter. The large flat seeds should be covered with

Dahlia 'Biddenham Blaze' (Small Decorative)

Dahlia 'Gerrie Hoek' (Small Decorative)

Dahlia 'Enfield Salmon' (Large Decorative)

Dahlia 'Lavendale' (Miniature Decorative)

compost, and kept in a propagator or in a warm position until germination, which does not usually take long. Prick out the seedlings into seed trays when large enough to handle. They grow large quite rapidly, so it may be necessary to start feeding them in the seed trays to prevent the seedlings from becoming starved.

Alternatively, divide a cluster of tubers carefully with a sharp knife, cutting through the old stem so that it is divided with tubers attached. Do not cut through the tuber itself. Dividing tubers is a very good method of increasing your stock if you do not have a greenhouse and a propagator in which to grow on cuttings.

If you have a greenhouse, and want as many daughter plants as possible, take cuttings. Start the tubers off on trays or boxes of moist peat or compost (there is no need to bury the tubers). Remove stem cuttings when they are 5cm (2in) high and

▲ *Dahlia* 'Diana Gregory' (Pompon)

▼ *Dahlia* 'Lady Linda' (Small Decorative)   ▼ *Dahlia* 'Biddenham Rust' (Miniature Ball)

Dahlia 'Old Harry' (Miniature Ball)

Dahlia 'Rose Willo' (Pompon)

root them in a warm, humid propagator after dipping the cuttings in a rooting hormone. If you don't have a propagator, use pots in a large polythene bag sealed at the top (make sure the cuttings do not touch the sides of the bag).

Pot up the cuttings individually once rooted, and harden off in late spring, ready for planting out in early summer.

POPULAR SPECIES

The true species are not grown, and the modern, highly bred dahlias that are available are divided into groups as a convenient way of describing them.

Dwarf bedding dahlias These usually have single or semi-double flowers and grow to 30–45cm (1–1½ft).

Decorative dahlias These have fully double blooms with slightly twisted ray florets. Giant decoratives produce flowers more than 25cm (10in) across; large decoratives have flowers between 20cm (8in) and 25cm (10in); medium decoratives have flowers between 15cm (6in) and 20cm (8in); small decoratives have flowers 10–15cm (4–6in) across; and miniature decoratives have

blooms less than 10cm (4in) across.

Cactus dahlias This type has fully double blooms with pointed, ray florets with a rolled edge. The sizes are similar to those given above for the decorative group.

Dahlia 'Nijinsky' (Ball)

Ball dahlias These have ball-shaped double blooms, like large pompons. Small ball varieties have flowers between 10cm (4in) and 15cm (6in) across and the miniature balls measure between 5cm (2in) and 10cm (4in) across.

Pompon dahlias These are similar to ball

Dahlia 'Jescot Julie' (Orchid-flowered)

Dahlia 'Comet' (Anemone-flowered)   *Dahlia* 'Ruwenzori' (Collerete)

varieties, but smaller and more rounded. They do not normally exceed 5cm (2in) in diameter.

Waterlily dahlias These, as their name suggests, have flowers rather like the shape of a waterlily, and are between 10cm (4in) and 15cm (6in) in diameter.

Collerette dahlias These have single outer florets and a central row of small florets on heads up to 10cm (4in) across.

Peony-flowered dahlias These have two or more rings of flat ray florets and a central disc on flowers measuring up to 10cm (4in) in diameter.

Anemone-flowered dahlias These have double flowers up to 10cm (4in) across with the flat outer florets surrounding a densely packed group of short tubular florets in the centre of the flower.

DRACUNCULUS

The genus name is Latin for little dragon, a description originally used by Pliny for a plant of now doubtful identity.

This is a flower to grow if you want to intrigue your friends. The genus has only a couple of species, and the one below is the most common. It is a tuberous-rooted plant that will spread to make a bold clump in a suitable spot – but don't plant it too near the house as the flowers have an unpleasant smell. It is uncommon and you will probably have to go to a specialist in uncommon bulbs to find it.

HOW TO GROW

Grow in a humus-rich soil in partial shade, planting the tubers to a depth of 15cm (6in). Leave the tubers undisturbed to form a substantial clump.

PROPAGATION

Lift an established clump in late summer and remove offsets before replanting.

POPULAR SPECIES

D. vulgaris (Mediterranean). This species has a maroon spathe with almost black spadix, flowering in early summer. Bold, lobed foliage. 1m (3ft) high.

E

ENDYMION
(Bluebell)

Bluebells are a traditional part of the European spring, and few can fail to be impressed by a large drift of them carpeting a woodland floor. But they have a place in the garden too. The strains that you buy from a bulb merchant are likely to be larger and bolder than the wild bluebells, and they needn't be invasive if you plant them in a suitable place. They thrive under trees and

Endymion hispanicus × nonscriptus

shrubs and are excellent for naturalizing in woodland (they will even grow under fir and pine trees). Try using them to clothe a bare shady spot.

There is a lot of confusion over the Latin nomenclature of the bluebells. You will probably find them listed in some bulb catalogues as endymion, in others as scillas.

HOW TO GROW

Plant immediately the bulbs become available, 3–5cm (1¼–2in) deep, in moist but not waterlogged soil; make sure it contains plenty of humus.

PROPAGATION

Lift, divide and replant established clumps as the leaves die down, otherwise sow seeds in shallow drills in a shady place once they ripen. If growing in a wild area of the garden, self-sown seedlings will probably appear anyway. Seedlings may take more than four years to flower.

POPULAR SPECIES

E. hispanicus (*Scilla hispanica, S. campanulata*). (W. and S. Europe, and N. Africa). Commonly known as the Spanish bluebell. The leaves are broader than the English bluebell, and the flowers larger. Apart from the various shades of blue, there are pink and also white varieties. 30–45cm (1–1½ft).

E. non-scriptus (*Scilla non-scripta, S. nutans*) (W. Europe, including Great Britain). This is the English bluebell. Grassy leaves and spikes of bluebells; there are also white and pink varieties. 30cm (1ft).

ERANTHIS
(Winter aconite)

he genus name comes from the Greek *er* (spring) and *anthos* (a flower), which reflects their flowering time.

These plants are always exciting to discover on a cold spring day, carpeting the ground with their bright yellow buttercup-like flowers set off by a green ruff. They can be difficult to establish, but once they have settled in conditions that they like, you can

be assured of a regular display for the minimum of attention.

If you have a small woodland area, try planting them in a fairly open patch of ground where they can establish a colony; if you don't, let them carpet the ground in front of shrubs, or simply naturalize them in an area of lawn, perhaps close to a specimen tree in the garden.

They don't demand shade, however, and can be very successful in, say, a planting pocket in a rock garden. They also make superb plants for growing in pots in an alpine house.

Because they are low growing and easy to miss in a remote part of the garden that you might not visit much in early spring, try to plant them near the house or a path, where they can be appreciated more easily.

HOW TO GROW

Eranthis require a good loam with plenty of humus that is also free draining. No fertilizer is required, but water regularly when they are growing and during very dry spells in the summer.

The tubers are sometimes reluctant to start into growth, so try soaking them in water for 24 hours before planting, about 5cm (2in) deep and 10cm (4in) apart, in autumn. Don't be surprised if the display is disappointing for the first season, but the display in future years will certainly be worth waiting for. Do not lift the tubers at the end

Eranthis cilicicus

Eranthis hyemalis

of the season.

Mulch with damp peat after flowering, provided the ground is already moist.

PROPAGATION

Divide well-established clumps in late summer, replanting the tubers without delay. The shock may affect flowering in the following spring, but they should bloom prolifically again the following year.

Alternatively, sow fresh seed in a cold frame in mid or late spring. The germination is likely to be slow and erratic. Grow the seedlings on for a couple of years then grow them on in rows in a nursery bed until ready for final planting. Seedlings take several years to reach flowering size.

POPULAR SPECIES

E. cilicicus (Asia Minor). Deep yellow buttercup-like flowers with a green ruff, in early or mid spring. 8cm (3in).
E. hyemalis (Europe). This is the winter aconite. Bright yellow buttercup-like flowers with a ruff of fringed leaves, in late winter and early spring. 8cm (3in).
E. pinnatifida (Japan). An uncommon, white-flowered species, blooming in early and mid spring. 8cm (3in).
E. × tubergenii (garden origin). Similar to the first two species, but with larger flowers that are sweetly scented. Early and mid spring. 10cm (4in).

ERYTHRONIUM

The name of the genus comes from the Greek word *erythronion*, from *erythros*, meaning red. The link is now obscure, and it was probably used to describe a plant that we can't now identify.

The erythroniums are sometimes dismissed as rather insignificant flowers by those who don't know them. Yet some of them are very showy, and even the small species are enchanting plants worth discovering.

They are most at home in a woodland setting, but look good in front of shrubs, or perhaps around the base of a specimen tree in the lawn. They produce a pretty display of flowers in spring, but some have attractively mottled foliage that makes them interesting for a longer period.

HOW TO GROW

Grow in partial or light shade, in humus-rich soil. Plant in autumn, covering the corms with about 5–8cm (2–3in) of soil, and spacing them 15–30cm (6–12in) apart, depending on the species or variety.

Once established they will come up dependably every year, and should not need any regular attention other than watering in dry spells in summer. This is especially important if they are in a dry position beneath trees.

Erythronium californicum

Erythronium dens-canis

Erythronium tuolumnense

PROPAGATION

Remove offsets when the plant is dormant, or sow seed as soon as it is ripe.

POPULAR SPECIES

E. americanum (E. USA). This is the trout lily, so-called because its mottled foliage resembles the markings on a trout. Bright yellow flowers in mid and late spring. 13cm (5in) high.

E. californicum (California). Creamy-white flowers in mid and late spring. Mottled leaves. 25cm (10in).

E. dens-canis (Europe to Japan). Commonly known as the dog's tooth violet because its long, shiny, white tuberous roots resemble a dog's tooth. Small nodding flowers not unlike cyclamen in shape, in shades of violet, pink, and white, in early spring. Mottled foliage. One of the easiest erythroniums to grow. 13cm (5in).

E. hendersonii (California, Oregon). Lavender flowers in mid spring. Dark, heavily mottled leaves. 25cm (10in).

E. oregonum (W. USA). Creamy-white flowers in mid and late spring. Marbled

Erythronium revolutum 'Pink Beauty'

foliage. 25cm (10in) high.

E. revolutum (W. USA). White or pink flowers up to 8cm (3in) across. 'White Beauty' has white flowers shading to pale yellow in the centre. Mid and late spring. 25cm (10in).

E. tuolumnense (California). Deep yellow flowers on slender stems in mid spring. 'Pagoda' is an especially good variety with sulphur yellow flowers. 25cm (10in).

EUCOMIS
(Pineapple flower or lily)

he genus name comes from the Greek *eu* (good) and *kome* (hair) (the flower spike has a terminal cluster of narrow leaf-like bracts which look like a head of hair).

These are distinctive plants that are not often grown in private gardens, but seldom fail to attract attention when they are seen. Except in very mild areas, it is best to grow them in a large pot, and keep in a cool greenhouse or conservatory for the winter.

HOW TO GROW

In a warm area, grow in a sunny, sheltered position, perhaps near the base of a sunny wall. Plant about 10cm (4in) deep in spring or autumn. Protect for the winter with a thick layer of coarse sand or pulverized bark.

Otherwise grow in large pots and stand outdoors for the summer if not required for

Erythronium oregonum 'White Beauty'

conservatory decoration.

PROPAGATION
Remove offsets in spring or autumn.

POPULAR SPECIES
E. bicolor (Natal, South Africa). Best grown in a greenhouse; stiff spikes of pale green flowers in mid summer. 60cm (2ft).
E. comosa (*E. punctata*) (South Africa). This species has strap-like foliage, stiff spikes of yellowish-white flowers on a purple-spotted stem, which bloom in late summer or early autumn. 60cm (2ft).

Eucomis comosa

F

FREESIA

Freesias need no introduction. Their powerful scent has ensured their popularity as cut flowers, and the best of the hybrids have relatively large and colourful flowers too, which adds to their value as decorative flowers in the home.

In mild areas, it's worth trying a few freesias in the garden. Grow them together with a low ground cover such as ajuga for winter protection. But the most satisfactory results come from pot-grown plants, or corms planted in a border or in a greenhouse to provide cut flowers.

HOW TO GROW
If growing outdoors, grow in a light, sandy soil and a sunny position. Buy a strain bred for this (your bulb catalogues will make it clear if they are suitable for growing outdoors). Plant the corms in mid spring to a depth of 5–8cm (2–3in) in a sheltered position and water freely in dry weather. Small twigy sticks will probably be necessary for support. For safety it is best to lift the corms in autumn and store them in a cool but frost-free place.

If growing in pots in a greenhouse, plant six corms to a 13cm (5in) pot. Don't try to grow them in the house – be content to move the pot indoors once the plants are in flower.

If you want freesias to flower from the end of January onwards, plant the corms in pots in early autumn, and plunge them into the ground in a cold frame, covering them with 2.5cm (1in) or so of moist peat. Towards the end of mid autumn (by which time the plants should have about seven leaves), the pots can be taken into the greenhouse and given full light. They will require a temperature of about 10°C 50°F), increased to about 16°C (60°F) after two weeks. The plants can be taken indoors when they begin to flower.

Freesia 'Red Star'

▲ *Freesia* 'Destiny'

PROPAGATION

Remove and grow on offsets; or raise from seed. Soak the seeds in water for 24 hours before sowing in early spring in a temperature of about 21°C (70°F). When large enough, prick out five or six seedlings into a 15cm (6in) pot and grow on in a cool greenhouse.

POPULAR SPECIES

The true species are not grown. The modern hybrids provide a much better colour range, larger flowers, and still plenty of fragrance.

Specialists offer named varieties, in shades of cream, white, yellow, scarlet, and blue. Double varieties are also available.

Consult seed and bulb catalogues for a selection of currently available varieties.

FRITILLARIA
(Fritillary)

These spectacular and beautiful plants are members of the lily family and are true bulbs. The name is derived from the Latin *fritillus* (a dicebox), due to the chequer-shaped markings of *F. meleagris*: dice were once associated closely with chequer or chess boards.

Fritillaria bulbs are very fragile and must be handled carefully, but the plants are long-lived and will multiply well, given the right conditions. They bloom for several weeks in spring. *F. imperialis* makes a bold display at the back of a border, or brightening up a shrubbery; *F. meleagris* looks pretty in sheltered corners and on rock gardens, or scattered through short turf. Most other species of fritillary are temperamental and some are probably best left to specialists. *F. imperialis* has a strange musky scent, which some people dislike. If you don't mind this, it makes an excellent cut flower.

HOW TO GROW

F. imperialis prefers a deep, rich and very moist soil: it likes sun but not dry conditions. The bulbs should be planted on their sides (or the hollow crowns will retain water, causing rotting) and covered with 15–

20cm (6–8in) of soil. Be careful, however, not to bruise them.

F. meleagris also loves moist conditions and flourishes in shade or sun. Plant the small bulbs 8cm (3in) deep.

All the other, less hardy species require very well-drained soil and a good deal of sun. If growing under glass, allow plenty of ventilation, even in winter.

Fritillaries object to being disturbed – *F. imperialis* is especially touchy – so try to avoid moving them for at least four years. Cut the stems down to ground level after they've died off, in summer.

Fritillaria imperialis

Fritillaria persica

Fritillaria imperialis

Fritillaria meleagris

PROPAGATION

Remove and replant offsets, or sow seeds.
The seed must be fresh, so don't leave too
long a gap between harvesting and planting.
Sow in 10–13cm (4–5in) pots, cover lightly
with compost, and keep in a cool greenhouse
or frame, well shaded. In winter, keep the
temperature at 5°C (41°F). Pick the
seedlings out in spring, about 10 to a pot,
and keep them protected under glass for
another year.

POPULAR SPECIES

F. acmopetala (Asia Minor). Bell-shaped
flowers, about 7cm (3in) long, coloured a
mixture of greens, purple and brown, in mid
spring. The leaves are linear. 30–45cm
(1–1½ft).
F. camtschatcensis (N.E. Asia, USA) Known
as the black lily. The deep purple-brown
flowers look almost black. They are bell-
shaped, open and pendant; late spring or
early summer. 30cm (1ft).
F. imperialis (N.E. Asia, USA) Commonly
called the crown imperial. Yellow, orange or
red flowers hang beneath a bright green
crown of green bracts, mid spring. The
variety 'Aurora' is fine and stately, with
bronze-orange flowers; 'Lutea Maxima' has
large brilliant golden-yellow flowers; 'Rubra
Maxima', one of the most vigorous and long-
lasting, has red flowers. 'Aureomarginata'
has glossy green leaves edged with yellow, in
whorls around the stem. 60–90cm (2–3ft).
F. meleagris (Europe, including Great
Britain). Popularly called the fritillary;
dainty, single or multiple flowers, checked
purple or white, or sometimes completely
white, in mid spring. The leaves are narrowly
lanceolate and grey-green. 30cm (1ft).
F. persica (Middle East). A good border
plant with large plum-purple bells in mid and
late spring. 'Adijaman' is the form usually
sold. 90cm (3ft).
F. pontica (S.E. Europe) Good for partial
shade. Green flowers tipped light brown;
late spring and early summer. 25cm (10in).
F. raddeana (Iran). Resembles a crown
imperial; green-yellow flowers, in early
spring. 75cm (2½ft) high.

Fritillaria meleagris

G

GALANTHUS
(Snowdrop)

The name combines the Greek *gala* (milk)
and *anthos* (a flower). Snowdrops arrive
in very early spring and will survive snowfall
unharmed; indeed, the flowers can resemble
drops of snow, poised on the low straps of
foliage. The white petals are nearly always
touched with green. Usually the flowers are
single with six petals, but there are doubles.

Galanthus nivalis 'Plena'

Snowdrops like growing in woods, under
shelter and in shade. Plant them in drifts for
best effect, between and among trees, in
grass or below a wall. Wild and hardy by
nature, they prefer cold and snow to sitting
indoors in pots. They combine very well with
small *Iris reticulata* and yellow winter
aconites (*Eranthis*).

Dried bulbs do not transplant very well,
and specialist nurseries may sell the plants
'in the green' after flowering, but don't be
deterred from trying dry bulbs as most
should still grow satisfactorily.

HOW TO GROW

Grow snowdrops preferably in woodland
conditions, in soil with a heavy loam, good
drainage, plenty of moisture and sun or
filtered shade. They need a good light from

Lift the clusters and separate them carefully into individual bulbs, each with its own roots and leaves. Replant the bulbs as soon as possible either among the old plants, or in a separate bed.

POPULAR SPECIES

G. elwesii (Asia Minor). A large-flowered species with snow-white, globular flowers, in early spring. The inner segments are marked a deep emerald green. The leaves are broad and strap-shaped. 15–25cm (6–10in).

G. nivalis (Europe). Known as the common snowdrop. The flowers are white, with blotches or streaks of green, depending on the variety, and appear in late winter or early spring. The leaves are strap-shaped and rather glaucous. Favourite varieties include the sweet-scented and vigorous 'Sam Arnott', the handsome 'Viridapicis' with its conspicuously green tipped petals, and the double 'Flore-plena'. 15cm (6in).

▲ *Galanthus* 'Mighty Atom'

▼ *Galanthus nivalis*

GALTONIA
(Summer hyacinth)

altonias were named after Sir Francis Galton, a nineteenth-century anthropologist. This genus contains just four bulbous species, only one of which is in general cultivation. It resembles the ordinary hyacinth to a slight extent, though galtonias are much larger, sparser in form and with a fainter scent. The tall stems carry numerous white pendant flowers, tinged with green at the base. The grey-green leaves are long and strap-shaped.

These plants make a bold show among shrubs, in the middle or at the back of a border, and will still be blooming in late autumn, when most other plants are past their best. They make striking and beautiful cut flowers.

Try galtonias in a large container for conservatory decoration.

HOW TO GROW

Plant the bulbs 15cm (6in) deep, and the same distance apart, in groups of at least three to five, either in mid autumn or in early or mid spring. Choose a sunny spot.

late winter through to mid spring.

Plant the bulbs 8–10cm (3–4in) apart, and cover them with 5cm (2in) of soil. Fertilizer is not necessary and will not, in fact, do a great deal of good.

PROPAGATION

Snowdrops will self-sow, if left to themselves, but it will be three to four years before the new plants flower. Alternatively you can collect the seed and sow it in pots or in a frame, under shade. Keep it well watered. If you buy seed, sow it between autumn and early spring.

Divide the plants just after the flowers have died, but while the foliage is still green.

Keep them moist and cover with a mulch in winter. Don't disturb them until they start to get crowded, when you can lift and replant. Remove the flower stems in autumn.

Galtonia candicans

PROPAGATION

Galtonias are difficult to grow from seed; it's easier to use offsets, removed from the bulbs in early autumn. These can be grown on like seedlings, near the parent plants, or potted up and overwintered under a cold frame, for planting outdoors in late spring.

POPULAR SPECIES

G. candicans (South Africa). Bell-shaped drooping white flowers with pale green markings on short stalks around a tall, erect stem; late summer. Slightly scented. The leaves are strap-shaped, arching and grow in rosettes around the base. 1.2m (4ft).

GLADIOLUS
(Sword lily)

he Latin word *Gladiolus* means a small sword, alluding to the sword-shaped leaves. These stunning cormous plants come in a great range of glowing colours and shades – yellow-white, salmon-orange, violet-blue, salmon-pink, golden-yellow and blood-scarlet, to name but a few. In general they have a narrow, upright growth habit.

Most gladioli now available are hybrids,

but there's no shortage of original species: botanists put the count at 300. New hybrids appear every year, in ever more lovely and vibrant colours.

Gladioli bloom in spring and summer, for about two weeks: by staggering planting times, you can keep a good show going over a long period. They are good border plants, but can look unnatural if planted singly or at the front of the border. Plant the large-flowered types in colour groups of about ten, behind bushy perennials. They make wonderful cut flowers, and are much beloved of florists and flower arrangers. Most start blooming about 100 days after planting, given clement weather conditions.

HOW TO GROW

Gladioli like sun and well-drained soil. Prepare the soil well before planting, by digging in manure or garden compost and raking in bonemeal. Peat will help to improve the soil structure.

The half-hardy hybrids should be planted in mid to late spring. If you want a succession of flowers, plant at three-weekly intervals, until early summer. Plant 10cm (4in) deep in heavy soil, or half as deep again in light soil, making sure the base of each corm is firmly set in the soil. Large-flowered types in particular must be planted at a good depth, or the plants may topple over in high winds when they've reached full height. You may have to stake the large-flowered hybrids, in which case be sure to attach the stake behind the stem, away from the flowers.

Lift gladiolus corms when the leaves turn yellow, in autumn, and before the first frost. Cut off the stem about 3cm (1½in) above each corm and brush away the soil. Throw away shrivelled corms.

Dry the corms for a couple of weeks in a well-ventilated greenhouse or room, then store in boxes or trays, in cool but not freezing conditions. Check them a few times during the winter.

Small gladioli can be grown in large pots, preferably in a peat compost with a third of grit or sand added. Plant the corms about 5cm (2in) deep in late autumn and give them a good initial watering: but then water very

▲ *Gladiolus byzantinus*

▼ *Gladiolus* 'Columbine' (Primulinus)

▲ *Gladiolus* × *colvillei*

Gladiolus 'Flower Song' (Large-flowered) ▶

sparingly until the shoots are through. They appreciate a fortnightly feed of liquid fertilizer.

PROPAGATION

Propagate from seed or offsets; either way, it will be two to three years before the plants flower. If you want to be sure of what you're getting, choose offsets – seeds often don't breed true to colour.

Plant the cormlets in spring, in drills about 8cm (3¼in) deep. Lift in autumn and store in the same way as corms; then plant them out again the next spring. Repeat this process the following year, or years. It is somewhat tedious, but worth it in the end.

Seeds should be sown in early spring. Sow the seeds thinly and shallowly, in trays. After the seedlings appear (usually in about five weeks), move the boxes to a cold frame. By early summer, they should be ready to face the open air. Keep them moist and feed occasionally with liquid manure.

POPULAR SPECIES

G. byzantinus (Turkey). This is hardier than most species gladioli. It bears magenta-red florets about 5cm (2in) across, in early summer, loosely arranged with the petals touching or overlapping. There is a pure white form, which makes a particularly good cut flower. 60cm (2ft).

G. × *colvillei*. Half-hardy. Scarlet flowers, 8cm (3¼in) across, with pointed petals, in early and mid summer. The lower flowers are usually yellow throated. Varieties include the pure white 'The Bride', and delicate pink 'Peach Blossom'. 45cm (1½ft).

Garden hybrids. The hybrids are much more commonly grown than the species. They can be divided into four main groups – large-flowered, primulinus, miniatures and butterflies.

Large-flowered hybrids have full, bright

florets, overlapping on a thick, tall flower stem, and all facing in one direction.

They are very vigorous, growing up to 1.2m (4ft), and produce flower spikes about 50cm (20in) long, from mid summer until early autumn. Varieties include salmon-pink and cream 'Dr Fleming', blood-red 'Life Flame', violet-purple 'Mabel Violet' and the pure white 'White Angel'.

In primulinus hybrids, the florets are more loosely arranged, and each has a hooded top petal. They are somewhat less vigorous in growth, although they flower freely. The flower spikes are 40cm (15in) long, with florets appearing in mid and late summer. The primulinus types have a slender, graceful habit of growth, and look very elegant in cut flower arrangements. Varieties include star-shaped 'Red Star' and 'Salmon Star' and brick-red 'Scarlet Knight'.

Gladiolus 'Oscar' (Large-flowered)

Gladiolus 'Greenbird' (Miniature)

The miniatures are similar, but smaller and neater with ruffled or frilled florets; 3–5cm (1½–2in). They flower in mid and late summer. Like primulinus types, they make excellent cut flowers. One particularly attractive variety is 'Greenbird', with light green, scarlet-throated florets. The butterfly hybrids are distinguished by their very striking throat markings and blotches. The florets are crowded together on a thick stem, to a length of 45cm (18in), from mid and late summer. Varieties include 'Madame Butterfly', which has pink flowers with salmon or violet throats, and 'Donald Duck', which has yellow-white flowers with deep orange-red blotches.

Gladiolus 'Melodie' (Butterfly)

GLORIOSA
(Climbing lily, glory lily)

The gloriosa lily lives up to its name – the flowers really are glorious. They are absolute eye-catchers, and especially impressive if you have never seen this unusual plant before. They are at their best climbing up a wall in a conservatory or in a large container in a greenhouse, but can be grown outdoors for the summer in many areas. You won't get a large plant covered with flowers in cool climates, but just a few of these flowers outdoors are striking enough to give you a sense of achievement.

Gloriosas can be grown as houseplants, but they need a very light position in order to flourish.

The common name of climbing lily says a lot about the plant. It is a member of the lily family and it does 'climb' – or more correctly cling with the tendrils that form at the ends of leaves. Given support (such as a trellis), it will reach about 1.8m (6ft). the red and yellow flowers resemble a Turk's cap lily.

HOW TO GROW

If planting outdoors make sure the soil is fertile and well drained, and that there is good light. Start the tubers into growth in a greenhouse or indoors first, planting out only after they have been thoroughly hardened off.

Place the long thin tubers horizontally on the compost and cover with about 8cm (3in) of compost. Even if you are planning to move the plants outside later, it is best to start the tubers in a large pot that you can plunge in the open ground later.

Initial staking and tying in may be necessary until the tendrils grasp the main support.

Keep the plants well watered throughout the growing season and feed regularly during the summer.

Once the foliage dies back, lift the tubers and store in dry peat or vermiculite.

PROPAGATION

Divide the tubers in spring, but make sure that each piece has an eye from which a shoot will grow (the eyes are easier to detect in spring).

Gloriosas can be grown from seed, but you will probably have to wait three or four years for flowers.

POPULAR SPECIES

G. rothschildiana (Tropical Africa). Bright red reflexed petals, yellow at the base and around the edge, in mid and late summer. 1.8m (6ft).

G. superba (Asia and Africa). Similar to previous species but more yellow, merging to orange and red, flowering in early summer to early autumn. 1.8m (6ft).

Gloriosa rothschildiana

H
HIPPEASTRUM
(Amaryllis)

ippeastrums are among the boldest and most magnificent bulbs that you can buy. They also have the merit of being very easy to grow too – which is why they make such popular gift plants.

The common name usually applied to these plants is amaryllis, which is confusing because there is another bulb, sometimes planted outdoors, that has the same name. Hippeastrum can only be grown indoors.

Hippeastrums are widely sold, often with a pot and compost, and sometimes ready-planted, in early winter. With even moderate care, you can expect them to flower for several years.

HOW TO GROW

Pot in a good potting compost, preferably with plenty of humus and good drainage (if necessary, add extra sand). Make a cone of compost in the bottom of a pot that is about 2.5cm (1in) wider than the bulb, put the bulb on top of this and spread the roots around the cone. Fill the pot with more compost, leaving half the bulb exposed. Soaking the base of the bulb and the roots in water for 24 hours may help it to grow away more quickly.

Adequate bottom heat is very important to start the big bulbs into growth. Water sparingly for the first couple of weeks, but once the shoot is emerging well, water freely (but never stand the pot in water).

Hippeastrums are sometimes 'prepared'

Hippeastrum Dutch hybrid

Hippeastrum 'Apple Blossom'

by special treatments to flower earlier (ideally for Christmas). To take advantage of this treatment, the prepared bulbs should be planted in mid or late autumn and a minimum temperature of 18°C (65°F) maintained day and night.

Bulbs planted between early and late autumn should flower from late winter, but it is possible to have hippeastrums in flower over a long period by planting treated and untreated bulbs at different times.

Cut off faded blooms when flowering is over, then start feeding with a liquid feed until late summer.

Rest the bulbs dry in their pots, and start watering again about five weeks before new growth is due to reappear. Annual repotting is not necessary.

PROPAGATION

Remove offset bulbs in autumn before new growth starts.

POPULAR SPECIES

Dutch hybrids (garden origin). The species are seldom grown, and it is the large hybrids that are commercially available. The large trumpet–shaped flowers come mainly in shades of red, pink, and white, early winter to late spring. 60–90cm (2–3ft).

HYACINTHUS
(Hyacinth)

Hyacinths manage to combine great beauty with a heady fragrance that can fill a room. They are popular subjects for forcing for early indoor blooming, but they are also excellent garden plants. Try them in containers or grow them in formal bedding schemes, or perhaps massed in beds or planted in informal groups in short grass around trees.

HOW TO GROW

For bowls or pots indoors, plant in autumn with the nose of the bulbs just above the surface. Prepared (treated) bulbs for early flowering must be planted as soon as possible once they become available if they are to flower for Christmas.

If using bowls without drainage use bulb fibre, but for pots with drainage any potting compost (or bulb fibre) can be used.

Keep the containers in a cool, shady spot outdoors, or in a cool, dark position indoors. If plunging them outdoors, slip a container without drainage holes into ventilated polythene bags (to prevent waterlogging and to keep them clean); cover with 15cm (6in) of peat or sand. Check periodically to ensure that the compost is not drying out.

Once the bulbs have formed a good root system and the shoots are showing, move them into a dark cupboard in a warm place indoors (aim for a temperature of 18–21°C (65–70°F), and water liberally.

When the flower bud stands well out of the neck (probably when the shoots are

Mixed hyacinths around a tree

Hyacinthus 'Ostara'

Hyacinthus 'Salmonette'

68cm (2½–3in high), bring the plants into a light position. Covering them with newspaper for a few days will encourage the flower shoots to lengthen if necessary.

Untreated bulbs naturally flower indoors over a period from mid winter to early spring, and by choosing early, mid season, and late varieties, it is possible to have hyacinths in flower over a long period.

Don't try to grow the bulbs indoors again for a second season. Plant them out in the garden to provide a less spectacular but nevertheless useful show in future years.

Outdoors, plant the bulbs about 10cm (4in) deep and 15cm (6in) apart, in full sun

▲ *Hyacinthus* 'Amsterdam'

▼ *Hyacinthus* 'Sky Jacket'

or partial shade. If used for formal bedding, lift and replant with new bulbs each year; left to naturalize they will provide a useful show in years to come.

PROPAGATION

Hyacinths are slow to multiply by natural methods, and growers use special techniques. Try making 10mm (½in) deep cuts like a cross in the base of the bulb, to stimulate formation of bulblets. These need to be grown on for several years before they reach flowering size. It is not an easy job for amateurs, but if you want to try, consult a specialist book on the subject.

Hyacinthus 'Lady Derby'

IPHEION

Only one species of this genus is sold commercially. This beautiful little plant may also be found under some of its synonyms (see below). It is a plant that may disappoint the first year, with just a couple of the small starry blue flowers appearing, but within a season or two the bulbs will have formed a clump that becomes a mound of quite long-lasting upward-facing flowers.

Try this plant in the rock garden, at the front of a border, in a gravel garden, or perhaps as an edging to a rose bed. It also makes a useful cold greenhouse or outdoor container plant provided the bulbs can be left undisturbed for at least a couple of years or so.

HOW TO GROW

Grow in well-drained soil in a sheltered position in sun or partial shade. Plant the

Ipheion uniflorum

bulbs 3–5cm (1–2in) deep, about 5–8cm (2–3in) apart in autumn, planting in a group whenever possible.

PROPAGATION

Lift an established clump as the leaves die down, divide it and replant as soon as possible. It is worth lifting and dividing a clump after about three years anyway.

POPULAR SPECIES

I. uniflorum (*Brodiaea uniflora, Triteleia uniflora*) (Peru, Argentina). Upward-facing blue star-like flowers on thin stems above grassy foliage, in early and mid spring. 13cm (5in) high.

IRISES

rises are a particularly pleasing and useful group of plants in a very large genus. The name iris comes from the Greek *iris*,

A border of bearded irises

meaning a rainbow – indicative of the wide colour range of these plants. Most species have typical iris-shaped flowers with standards (upward-pointing petals) and falls (downward-pointing petals), but in nature many of them grow in very diverse habitats, and there are species suitable for the rock garden, water garden, bog garden, border, and show bench. Some have rhizomes, others are true bulbs.

Most irises have a relatively short flowering period, but by growing a range of

Iris danfordiae

Iris germanica hybrid

species and varieties which follow each other in succession it is often possible to extend the season of interest. The border irises especially are so bold and colourful that it is worth finding space for them even if they are uninteresting for eleven months of the year. They are best in groups in a mixed or herbaceous border. These irises are also effective planted in drifts in front of shrubs.

The species listed here are only a representative selection of the most popular kinds sold by bulb merchants, but specialist nurseries will be able to offer a much wider range of species.

The bearded border irises (bearded irises have a 'beard' in the centre of the upper part of the falls), are at their most magnificent in a border of their own. Spectacular though they are in early summer, however, such a border will look boring for the rest of the year. Unless you have a large garden with enough space to devote to single-subject borders, they are best in groups in a mixed or herbaceous border.

Most bulbous irises sold by bulb merchants are spring-flowering. They are relatively inexpensive, bright, and dependable for first-year flowering. Don't expect such a good repeat performance the next spring, however, as they tend to split up into a number of small bulbs that may take a year or two to make bigger and bolder flowering clumps.

The summer-flowering Dutch, Spanish and English bulbous irises are well known as cut flowers but are less commonly used in the border. They are, however, very useful border plants for early and mid summer bloom. Each type flowers about a fortnight later than the previous one; by growing all three kinds the period of interest can be expanded to over a month.

HOW TO GROW •

Plant those with rhizomes in a sunny position in mid autumn. Most prefer a light soil, and many do well on limy ground. The rhizomes should be planted with the top half exposed, in groups about 25cm (10in) apart.

The most popular types of bulbous irises are not fussy about soil. All the types listed below can be left in the ground to form large clumps. Plant *I. reticulata* and *I. danfordiae* about 5cm (2in) deep, and the *I. xiphium* hybrids 10–15cm (4–6in) deep, in autumn.

PROPAGATION

The easiest way to increase bearded border irises is to divide the rhizomes in mid summer, after flowering. Lift the clumps and then divide the rhizomes with a sharp knife. Each piece should be about 10–15cm (4–6in) long with one or more fans of foliage.

The bulbous types are easily propagated from offsets. Lift an established clump after the foliage has died down. Replant the largest bulbs where they are to flower the

Iris xiphium

Iris reticulta

following year, and grow on the smaller ones in a nursery bed for a year or two before planting out in their flowering positions in late autumn.

Irises can be raised from seed, but it's a slow business, and the seedlings also take several years to reach flowering size.

POPULAR SPECIES

I. danfordiae (E. Turkey). Bulbous type; fragrant yellow flowers open as the leaves emerge, in late winter. 10cm (4in).
I. pumila hybrids (garden origin). Rhizome. These dwarf bearded irises are low-growing but have large flowers 8–10cm (3–4in) across. 10–25cm (4–10in).
I. germanica hybrids (garden origin). Rhizome known as intermediate bearded irises; flowers 8–10cm (3–4in) across, in late spring. 25–75cm (10–30in).
I. pallida hybrids (garden origin). Rhizome; tall bearded irises, with flowers 10–15cm (4–6in) across, in late spring or early summer. 75cm–1.5m (2½–5ft).
I. reticulata (Russia, Caucasus, N. Persia). Bulbous type; blue or purple flowers opening among elongating narrow ribbed leaves, in late winter and early spring. There are several varieties in varying shades of blue and purple. 15cm (6in).

▽ *Iris pallida* 'Aurea-variegata'

Iris tuberosa

Iris pumila 'Pogo'

Iris pumila 'Blue Denim'

I. tuberosa (*Hermodactylus tuberosus*) (Levant). Unusual purple-black and green flowers in mid spring. 30cm (10ft).

I. xiphioides (Pyrenees) Commonly called the English iris; bulbous type; usually blue flowers, with gold blaze on petals, in mid summer. 60cm (2ft).

I. xiphium hybrids (France, Portugal, S. Spain, N.W. Africa) Also called Dutch or Spanish irises; bulbous types; blue, purple, white, or yellow flowers on stiff stems early and mid summer. 30–60cm (1–2ft).

IXIA
(African corn lily)

The name comes from the Greek world ixia, or bird lime, and refers to the sticky sap exuded by the plant. Only two species are in cultivation. The hybrids are more commonly used, however, and are certainly more vigorous.

The star-shaped flowers are borne on long thin stems and bloom for several weeks in late spring and early summer. They are colourful in both bud and flower, the most common colours being rose, red, orange, yellow or cream. The leaves are sword-shaped, borne in a narrow fan.

Ixias make such good cut flowers (usually lasting for more than a week), but you should put the stems in water as soon as

Ixia viridiflora

possible: if the stems are exposed to the air for too long, the flowers will close up and refuse to reopen.

HOW TO GROW

Most of the species are not hardy in cool areas; they are much more suitable for growing in pots in a cool greenhouse or indoors (but make sure they get plenty of sunlight). If you want to risk them outdoors, they like dry conditions, a sunny and sheltered spot, and well-drained soil, preferably sandy.

Plant the corms in mid or late autumn, covering them with 8–10cm (3–4in) of soil. If you want them for cutting, plant in rows about 40cm (16in) apart; otherwise plant in groups, in a sunny border. Protect them from frost under cloches, or lay down a thick layer of bracken or coarse sand.

If growing in pots under glass, plant five corms to a 13cm (5in) pot, about 5cm (2in) deep, and keep fairly dry until the plants begin to show some growth. Don't let the temperature drop below 13°C (55°F), for early spring flowering.

Dead-head the flowers leaving only the lower part of the stalk. When the leaves are dead too, remove the plants from their pots and store the corms in a dry, frost-proof place until it's time to plant again.

PROPAGATION

Detach the cormlets and plant them separately, or you can save the seeds and sow them under glass in spring, at a temperature of about 16°C (61°F). The seedlings will take about two years or so to flower.

POPULAR SPECIES

I. viridiflora (South Africa). This species is best grown under glass. It has vibrant blue-green flowers, with a very dark almost black centre, about 4cm (1½in) wide. *I. viridiflora* appears in late spring and early summer. 30cm (1ft) high.

Garden hybrids (garden origin). These are hardier, more colourful, and come in shades of yellow, red, purple and white (usually with a contrasting centre) in late spring and early summer. 45cm (1½ft).

IXIOLIRION

The name combines the Greek *ixia* with *lirion* (a lily). Unlike ixias, these are true bulbs. There are several species, all quite similar. They usually bear clusters of star-shaped violet-blue flowers in profusion and look very attractive in cut flower arrangements in the home.

Ixiolirions can be difficult to grow outdoors in cold areas, despite their Siberian origins. They like a warm sheltered spot and plenty of sun. The foliage is spindly and grasslike and disappears quickly, so they are ideal bulbs to grow in borders through ground-cover plants.

Ixiolirion tartaricum

HOW TO GROW

Grow in well-drained soil, in a sunny, sheltered position. Plant in autumn, or in early spring if your area is cold. For a good display, plant 5–8cm (2–3in) apart, in groups. You can also grow ixiolirions in pots in a cool greenhouse.

PROPAGATION

Dig up the bulbs carefully in autumn, separate the small bulblets and replant.

POPULAR SPECIES

I. tataricum pallassi (*I. pallasii*) (Siberia). This species has violet-blue, star-shaped flowers carried in a loose cluster at the top of the thin stems, in early summer. 30–45cm (12–18in).

L

LEUCOJUM
(Snowflake)

These are very adaptable and easy bulbs to grow. They resemble snowdrops, but grow much taller.

These are plants that are best left undisturbed to form large clumps in a mixed border or perhaps near the edge of a pool.

Although you should be able to purchase some of the species from most bulb merchants, expect them to take a season to settle down, as they resent disturbance and drying off in the summer.

HOW TO GROW

Plant as soon as the bulbs are available, in late summer or early autumn. Plant *L. aestivum* and *L. vernum* in a moisture-retentive soil, in sun or partial shade. *L. autumnale* prefers free-draining ground in full sun. Plant the first two about 8cm (3in) deep and 5–10cm (2–4in) aparts, and *L. autumnale* about 5cm (2in) deep.

Leucojum vernum

▲ *Leucojum aestivum*

PROPAGATION

Every few years lift and divide an established clump and replant some of the offsets together with some of the larger bulbs.

POPULAR SPECIES

L. aestivum (Central and S.E. Europe). Known as the summer snowflake; produces white nodding bells, tipped green, in mid and late spring. 'Gravetye' is an improvement on the species, being more robust and free-flowering. 60cm (2ft).

L. autumnale (Iberian peninsula, Mediterranean islands, N. Africa). Narrower leaves than the other two species, and not such a bold plant, but flowers from late summer to mid autumn. 15–23cm (6–9in).

L. vernum (C. Europe). White nodding bell flowers, tipped green (tipped yellow in the variety 'Carpathicum'), blooming in late winter or early spring. Strap-shaped arching foliage. 23cm (9in) high.

LILIUM
(Lily)

There are probably thousands of varieties of lily cultivated around the world. Only a few basic kinds can be discussed have, but most good bulb catalogues will offer advice

Lilium 'Corsage'

about the range of varieties that they stock.

Although a few true species are grown, the vast majority of those offered by bulb merchants or those you will find in garden centres will be hybrids.

You can grow lilies in pots outdoors, and they make excellent patio or conservatory plants treated this way.

To cope with the wide range of lilies available, varieties are generally put into one of nine categories or 'divisions' (there are also sub-divisions): asiatic hybrids, martagon hybrids, candidum hybrids, American

hybrids, longiflorum hybrids, trumpet and aurelian hybrids, Oriental hybrids, hybrids not belonging to any other division, and true species and botanical varieties.

HOW TO GROW

If planting in pots or tubs, plant with about 5–8cm (2–3in) of soil above the bulbs; use any good potting compost (a peat-based compost may be too light to support the tall top growth in a small pot), or make up a compost composed of one part loam, peat, leaf-mould, and coarse sand (and if you can

Lilium speciosum hybrid

Lilium 'Imperial Gold'

Lilium 'Enchantment'

Lilium 'Yellow Star' ▶

get it – well-decayed cow manure).

Pot-grown lililes are often sold in shops in flower as houseplants. They are well worth buying for indoor decoration if you are prepared to plant them outdoors afterwards. Don't expect to be able to grow such compact plants indoors yourself. The ones you see in the shops have been specially treated with chemicals; if you try to grow and flower them indoors yourself, you will almost certainly have a disappointing display of lanky and not very attractive plants.

The most satisfactory long-term home for lilies is in the ground outdoors. Plant the bulbs in autumn or early spring, but if the bulbs look shrivelled try keeping them in trays of moist peat for a few days first. Basal-rooting lilies are generally best planted in autumn.

Most lilies grow in sun or partial shade and prefer well-prepared deeply dug soil. Add plenty of garden compost, peat, and grit if possible. Some species require a lime-free soil to do well, but others are much more tolerant.

The best planting depth will depend on the individual species or variety. As a guide, plant bulbs in groups and cover the bulbs with their own depth of soil. Stem-rooting kinds (roots come from the stem above the bulb as well as from the base) should be planted a bit deeper. *L. candidum* is planted just below the surface. Most kinds are best planted about 30cm (1ft) apart, though this depends on the species or hybrid.

Mulch the plants and add a general fertilizer each spring if possible. Leave undisturbed to form established clumps.

Lilium 'Imperial Silver'

Lilium 'Citronella'

Keep them moist during the growing season and do not let them dry out completely even when they are resting.

Although plants grown in tubs or pots will almost certainly require staking, those planted in the ground should not require support as long as they are planted in a sheltered spot in the garden.

PROPAGATION

You can raise the species from seed but it's a slow and sometimes difficult job. It is better to use one of the alternative methods.

Bulbils (small bulbs) are produced in the leaf joints of some species (*L. tigrinum* is one of them), and these can be removed as the foliage turns yellow. Pot these up in a frame, and grow them on for two or three years before planting in their final positions.

Offset bulbs provide the easiest method of propagation. Remove small bulblets from the parent bulb in late summer. The largest of these can be planted out and the smaller ones treated as bulbils.

If you want a lot of bulbs, separate the scales from healthy bulbs in early autumn or

Lilium 'Cornish Hybrids'

 Lilium martagon

 Lilium auratum

Lilium regale

Lilium pardalinum

Lilium 'Pink Pearl'

Lilium × *testaceum*

spring, and put them into a polythene bag containing damp horticultural vermiculite (it's worth dipping the scales into a fungicide first). Place the bag in a warm place (about 10–13°C/50–55°F), until plantlets can be seen forming on the scales. Pot these up singly and grow on as described for bulbils.

POPULAR SPECIES

L. auratum (Japan). Known as the golden-rayed lily. Large white spreading petals, striped yellow and spotted purple, as much

Lilium henryi

Lilium candidum

as 25cm (10in) across, in late summer and early autumn. Fragrant. There are several varieties. Stem-rooting; requires a lime-free soil. 1.8m (6ft).

L. candidum (Asia Minor). Popularly called the madonna lily; trumpet-shaped fragrant white flowers about 8cm (3in) long, in early and mid summer. 1.5m (5ft).

L. henryi (China). This species has pale apricot yellow flowers spotted red, in late summer and early autumn. Stem-rooting; lime-tolerant 1.8m (6ft) high.

 Lilium 'Golden Splendour'

▼ *Lilium longiflorum*   ▼ *Lilium* 'Damson'

Lilium trigrinum

L. longiflorum (Japan). Fragrant white trumpets, mid and late summer. 90cm (3ft).
L. martagon (Albania, Eastern Europe). Called the Turk's cap lily; pale or dark purple nodding flowers with reflexed petals with dark spots, in mid summer. There are white and pink forms; lime-tolerant. 1.2m (4ft).
L. pardalinum (Calitornia). Orange-red 'turk's cap' flowers, spotted purple-brown, in mid summer. Requires lime-free soil. 1.5m (5ft).
L. regale (China). Large white fragrant trumpets with a yellow base, flushed lilac-mauve to purple outside, in mid summer. Stem-rooting. 1.5m (5ft).
L. speciosum (Japan). Nodding, white, fragrant flowers with reflexed petals, shaded crimson, in late summer. There are several varieties and hybrids. Stem-rooting. Requires lime-free soil. 1.5m (5ft) high.
L. × testaceum (garden origins). This species has pale yellow flowers in mid and late summer. 1.5m (5ft).
L. trigrinum (China, Korea, Japan). Known as the tiger lily. Orange-scarlet, strongly reflexed flowers, spotted purple-black, in late summer and early autumn. Stem-rooting; forms bulbils in the leaf axils. Requires lime-free soil. 1.5m (5ft).
Garden hybrids (garden origin). It is best to consult a specialist catalogue if you want to grow the hybrids. Try the Mid-Century Hybrids to start with. These have dense heads of flowers about 10cm (4in) across, ranging from yellow through orange to red. There are named varieties such as 'Destiny' (yellow, spotted brown) and 'Enchantment' (orange). 1–1.12m (3–4ft).

M

MORAEA

You will have to search the specialist catalogues to find moraeas, and they are not always reliable in cool, wet climates, but they have that exotic look that makes them worth trying for something different. Individual blooms are very short-lived, so there should be a succession of them.

HOW TO GROW

Grow in a light, sandy soil, preferably in full sun in a warm, sheltered position. Plant about 3–5cm (1–2in) deep in spring. Lift in autumn and store in a frost-free place for the winter.

PROPAGATION

Separate offsets when replanting.

POPULAR SPECIES

M. iridioides (South Africa). Three-petalled yellow and white flowers in summer. 45cm (1½ft). 'Johnsonii' is a stronger, taller form. 60cm (2ft).
M. latifolium (Turkey). Spikes of pale blue flowers, more purple-blue in the lower part, in mid spring. 23cm (9in).
M. macrocarpum (Turkey). An unusual species with fragrant yellow flowers in spring. 15–20cm (6–8in).
M. spathulata (*M. spathacaea*) (South Africa). An uncommon species. Yellow, fragrant flowers in summer. 60–90cm (2–3ft).

MUSCARI
(Grape hyacinth)

The genus name is derived from a Turkish word for the sweetly aromatic scent of the flowers of one of the species; this, in turn, is derived from the Persian word *mushk*, or testicle, referring to musk. These are among the easiest and most trouble-free bulbs. Most are inexpensive, very easy to grow, and can be depended upon to flower well every year: a good garden investment.

Try grape hyacinths in the rock garden, in small drifts at the front of a herbaceous or shrub border, or as an edging to a bed. Left undisturbed, each bulb soon forms a small clump and the edging will become dense and showy. In comparison with most other bulbs the grassy foliage is present for a long time.

HOW TO GROW

Plant the bulbs about 8cm (3in) deep and 10cm (4in) apart, in a sunny position. Once planted, leave them alone to multiply.

PROPAGATION

Lift established clumps and replant the largest bulbs in their flowering positions; grow the smaller ones on for a season or two until they become established.

Muscari azureum

Muscari armeniacum 'Blue Spike'

Muscari tubergenianum

POPULAR SPECIES

M. armeniacum (S.E. Europe, W. Asia). Densely packed spikes of blue flowers in mid and late spring. 'Blue Spike' is a double-flowered variety. 23cm (9in).

M. azureum (Asia Minor). Azure blue flowers in early spring. 15cm (6in).

M. botryoides (C. Europe). Small spikes of sky blue flowers in spring. 20cm (8in).

M. latifolium (Turkey). Purple flowers in mid and late spring. 23cm (9in).

M. macrocarpum (Turkey). Yellow flowers in mid and late spring. 15cm (6in).

M. tubergenianum (Persia). The Oxford and Cambridge muscari; each flower is coloured light and dark blue. 15cm (6in).

▲ *Muscari latifolium*

▼ *Muscari macrocarpum*

NARCISSUS
(Daffodils and narcissi)

Narcissi are among the most widely planted bulbs, and the trumpet varieties popularly known as daffodils are to be seen everywhere in spring.

There are many kinds, from dainty miniatures for the rock garden or to be grown in pots in an alpine house, to the big bold yellow trumpet kinds.

They are divided horticulturally into 11

groups, each with their own characteristics. The group number is often given in catalogues for easy reference.

Division 1: trumpet daffodils (the old 'King Alfred' is the most famous, but varieties such as 'Dutch Master' are much better). Division 2: large-cupped narcissi (the cup is more than a third, but less than a length, of the perianth segment; 'Fortune' is a good yellow with orange cup). Division 3: small cupped narcissi (the cup is less than one-third of the perianth segment; 'Aflame' is an old but excellent variety with a cream perianth and deep red cup). Division 4: doubles ('Irene Copland' is a fully double variety with creamy-white and apricot

▲ *Narcissus* 'Sweetness' (Div. 7)
◀ *Narcissus* 'Dutch Master' (Div. 1)
▼ *Narcissus* 'Bartley' (Div. 6)

 *Narcissus* 'Trevithian' (Div. 7)

Narcissus pseudo-narcissus

Narcissus rupicola

Narcissus × *odorus* 'Rugulosus'

flowers). Division 5: triandrus narcissi (these have more than one flower to a stem and often hang down; 'Thalia' is a good white variety). Division 6: dwarf cyclamineus narcissi (the perianth is reflexed like a cyclamen; 'February Gold' is an excellent

Narcissus bulbocodium

Narcissus 'Ardour' (Div. 3)

very early deep yellow hybrid). Division 7: jonquilla narcissi (more than one flower to a stem and usually fragrant; 'Suzy' is an excellent variety with bright yellow perianth and small orange cup). Division 8: tazetta daffodils (many strongly scented flowers in a cluster; 'Minnow' is a charming dwarf with lemon yellow perianth and flat yellow cups). Division 9: poeticus narcissi (a large white perianth and small cup; the old 'Pheasant Eye' is still one of the best, with its small deep red eye set off against a large white perianth). Division 10: species and wild forms, and their close hybrids (including such charming miniatures as *N. bulbocodium conspicuous*, the yellow hoop petticoat narcissus). Division 11: any other form not included above (such as split cup varieties).

The dwarf kinds are excellent in rock gardens or windowboxes and other containers, and some of them, such as the hoop petticoat narcissus, do well naturalized in short grass. It is generally the larger kinds that are naturalized, however, and these can be left unattended for many years. Daffodils are particularly good for growing under

Narcissus 'Actaea' (Div. 9)

deciduous trees, but they are equally successful planted in bold drifts in front of shrubs or in small groups in herbaceous or mixed borders. They are often planted in regimented rows in a border, but they seldom look as impressive like this; it is best to grow them in informal groups or drifts where they can be left to multiply into big, bold clumps.

HOW TO GROW

Cover the bulbs with about twice their own

Narcissus poeticus

Narcissus 'Fortune' (Div. 2)

Narcissus 'Duke of Windsor' (Div. 2)

Narcissus 'Texas' (Div. 4)

Narcissus 'Mary Copeland' (Div. 4)

Narcissus triandus

Narcissus 'Mount Hood' (Div. 1)

depth of soil, though this is not critical. They do well in sandy loams, but will grow in most soils provided they are not waterlogged. Give a light dressing of a general balanced fertilizer in spring, but do not overfeed the soil with nitrogen.

The leaves can look untidy when flowering is over, but let them die down naturally. If the plants are in a bed where you feel unable to leave them, lift and replant the bulbs in a spare piece of ground until the leaves die off naturally.

Try to avoid cutting the grass where daffodils are naturalized for at least a month after they have flowered. Cutting the foliage too soon will reduce the number of flowers

Narcissus 'Rippling Waters' (Div. 5)

Narcissus cyclamineus

the following year.

PROPAGATION

Lift and divide an established clump and replant the offsets as soon as possible. Even small offsets should bloom in about three years, larger offsets should flower even more quickly.

POPULAR SPECIES

The majority of narcissi offered by garden centres and bulb merchants are hybrids, and it is best to consult bulb catalogues if you want a list of the many varieties.

Representatives of the many small species are *N. bulbocodium*, yellow, 15cm (6in), late winter; *N. × odorus* 'Rugulosus',

Narcissus triandus albus

a jonquil with about four flowers to a stem, 25cm (10in), early and mid spring; *N. cyclamineus*, good for naturalizing, 15cm (6in), late winter and early spring; *N. rupicola* has solitary, relatively large flowers, 10cm (4in), blooming in mid spring; *N. pseudo-narcissus* has pale yellow flowers, good for naturalizing, 15cm (6in), flowering in early spring; A larger species is the pheasant's eye narcissus *N. poeticus*, which has a tiny yellow cup edged red in the centre of snow-white swept-back petals.

NERINE

These attractive plants, with their heads of usually pink spidery flower, are named after a princess of Grecian mythology.

They are especially worth the effort to grow well because they flower in autumn and produce their best display when most other plants have finished. The one drawback to these plants is that they are not dependably hardy, although the tougher kinds, such as *N. bowdenii*, can safely be left outdoors for the winter in the milder areas.

As they flower well when rootbound, they make excellent pot plants for the patio, cool greenhouse or conservatory.

HOW TO GROW

Nerine bowdenii is the species to try overwintering outdoors. Plant in mid spring or early autumn in any ordinary well-drained soil, in a warm position, preferably near a sunny wall. Cover the bulbs with about 10cm (4in) of soil, spaced about 30cm (1ft) apart.

Leave undisturbed if possible, and only lift and divide every four or five years when

Nerine bowdenii

the clumps become too congested.

It may be worth covering the ground with a layer of straw for the winter if you want to reduce the chances of losses if it becomes very cold.

The more tender kinds can be potted up in early autumn, with the neck of the bulb just showing through a loam-based compost. Start to water at first sign of the flower buds appearing, and keep just moist throughout the winter. Maintain a minimum temperature of 10°C (50°F), and feed with a liquid fertilizer when the foliage has developed, and regularly until it turns yellow. Keep the pots in a bright position.

PROPAGATION
Remove and replant offset bulbs when dividing an established clump.

POPULAR SPECIES
N. bowdenii (Cape Province). This is the most widely planted species. Heads of up to eight spidery pink flowers from early to late autumn. 'Fenwick's Variety' is a particularly good form. 45cm (1½ft).

N. flexuosa (South Africa). A tender species with pink flowers on thin stems, in autumn. 'Alba' is a white form. 60cm (2ft).

N. sarniensis (Cape Province). Known as the Guernsey lily. A tender species grown outdoors in the Channel Islands for many years. Heads of pale pink to red flowers in early to late autumn. 60cm (2ft).

ORNITHOGALUM

The name is derived from the Greek words *ornis* (a bird) and *gala* (milk); the term bird's milk was said to be a current expression among the ancient Greeks for some wonderful thing.

Only a few species of this low-growing plant are grown in gardens. The flowers are white or a very pale green, and are a refreshing and attractive sight to encounter in spring.

Try growing the hardy species in short grass, or in the rock garden.

HOW TO GROW
Plant in groups in the autumn (except *O. thyrsoides*), spacing the bulbs about 8–10cm (3–4in) apart and covering with 3–5cm (1–2in) of soil. They will grow equally successfully in full sun or partial shade. They should require no regular attention.

PROPAGATION
The seed usually germinates readily, but unless you want a lot of plants, and are prepared to wait a couple of years for them to flower, use the bulb offsets. Lift an

Ornithogalum umbellatum

Ornithogalum arabicum

Ornithogalum balansae

established plant when the leaves die down, and replant the offsets.

POPULAR SPECIES

O. arabicum (Mediterranean). This species is best grown in pots. Small, glistening, pearly white flowers with a dark centre appear in late spring and early summer. 45cm (1½ft) high.

O. balansae (Asia Minor). Star-shaped flowers striped green on the outside, in early and mid spring. 15cm (6in).

O. nutans (Europe). Quite large, bell-shaped, silver-grey and pale green flowers in mid and late spring. 30cm (1ft).

O. thyrsoides (South Africa). Known as the chincherinchee: an exceptionally good cut flower, best grown in a cool greenhouse in spring. Densely packed spikes of white buds opening to reveal a brown centre and yellow stamens, from late spring to mid summer. 45cm (1½ft).

O. umbellatum (Europe, N. Africa). Popularly called the star of Bethlehem. Star-shaped, rather flat, pure white flowers in late spring. 10cm (4in).

Ornithogalum nutans

OXALIS

he name comes from the Greek *oxys* (acid) alluding to the acidity of the leaves of many species.

Some oxalis are noxious weeds difficult to eradicate from the garden, but there are also some charming and useful plant's for rock gardens in this large genus. Only a few of them will be found in bulb catalogues.

HOW TO GROW

These plants are not fussy about soil, but require full sun. Plant them 5–15cm (2–6in) apart, covering the bulbs with about 3cm (1in) of soil.

Water if the ground becomes very dry during the growing season, otherwise they require no regular attention.

PROPAGATION

Lift an established plant and replant the offsets.

POPULAR SPECIES

O. adenophylla (Chilean Andes). Fan-shaped grey-green foliage. Pink flowers with dark eyes in late spring. Best in the rock garden. 10cm (4in).
O. deppei (Mexico). Sometimes called the lucky clover or good luck plant, it resembles a four-leaf clover with a dark blotch at the base of each petal. Another common name is the iron cross oxalis. Pink flowers, mid

summer to early autumn. 15cm (6in).
O. pes-caprae (*O. cernus*) (South Africa). Bright, showy drooping yellow flowers in spring and autumn. Spreads rapidly so needs careful placing. 23cm (9in).

Oxalis pes-caprae

Oxalis adenophylla

Oxalis deppei

P
PUSCHKINIA
(Striped squill)

The genus is named after Appollos Mussin-Puschkin, a Russian botanist.

Only one species is likely to be available commercially. It is a useful plant to naturalize in short grass, or group in small clumps in the rock garden. It also makes a charming plant in pots in an alpine house or a cool greenhouse.

HOW TO GROW

Plant in autumn in free-draining soil in full sun or partial shade. It will do well in gritty soil in a rock garden. Plant them in groups or drifts, 5–8cm (2–3in) apart, with about 5–8cm (2–3in) of soil over the bulbs. Leave undisturbed.

PROPAGATION

Can be raised from seed sown when ripe, usually about early summer. They will take about three years to reach flowering size.

Offset bulbs should be quicker. Lift an established clump and replant the offsets.

POPULAR SPECIES

P. libanotica (*P. scilloides*) (W. Asia). Clusters of pale blue flowers with a deeper blue stripe along centre of petals, in early and mid spring. 10cm (4in) high.

Puschkinia libanotica

R
RANUNCULUS

The name of the genus comes from the Latin *rana* (frog), referring to the wet habitat of many species, though it does not apply to the species mentioned here.

HOW TO GROW

Plant in early spring, claws downwards, about 10cm (4in) deep and 15cm (6in) apart. It is worth mixing sand or grit in the planting area unless the soil is already free-draining. Autumn planting is possible (for early flowering), but it is unwise outdoors except in the mildest areas. Spring planting should produce flowers during the summer months.

If growing in a cool greenhouse, plant in the border to provide cut flowers.

In all but the mildest areas outdoors, lift the tubers when the leaves have turned yellow. Dry them off in the sun and store in a frost-proof place for the winter.

PROPAGATION

The tubers can be divided, but they are brittle and must have a bud attached if they are to grow. They are also easy to raise from seed, and some strains will flower within six months of sowing under ideal conditions. The results may be variable, however, and you probably won't have as many good doubles as you would from bought tubers.

Ranunculus asiaticus

POPULAR SPECIES

R. asiaticus (Asia Minor). The true species is unlikely to be grown, and it is the double hybrids that are of garden value. 'Tecolote' is an outstanding mixture. The flowers resemble miniature peonies and come in shades of red, pink, orange, yellow, and white, in early summer. 30cm (1ft).

RHODOHYPOXIS

The name rhodophypoxis comes from the Greek *rhodo* (red) and *Hypoxis* (the name of an allied genus).

This is a small genus with only a couple of species, just one of which is usually sold. It has corm-like rhizomes. It is sold either as pot-grown plants by alpine suppliers or as a dried rhizome by bulb merchants.

It makes an excellent pot plant for a cool greenhouse or alpine house, and is well worth having in the rock garden.

HOW TO GROW

Plant in autumn in a sunny position, about 3cm (1in) apart; cover with 12–25mm (½–1in) of soil. If growing in pots, use a free-draining loam-based compost. Either way, leave undisturbed for a few years to form a bold clump.

PROPAGATION

Lift an established clump in autumn and divide the rootstock. Most of the offsets should flower the following year.

Rhodohypoxis baurii

POPULAR SPECIES

R. baurii (South Africa). Small star-shaped flowers, from white to deep pink, above tufts of grass-like foliage, in mid and late summer. 7.5cm (3in).

ROSCOEA

You will have to search the catalogues for these strange plants, which are named after William Roscoe, a founder member of the Liverpool Botanic Garden. The flowers have three petal-like lobes, the upper one larger and erect or hooded, and a broad petal-like staminode equivalent to the labellum of an orchid. They grow best in a rock garden or at the front of a border.

HOW TO GROW

Grow in a humus-rich soil in sun or partial shade, to a depth of 8–10cm (3–4in). May require winter protection. Planting deeply will help.

PROPAGATION

Sow seed in a cold frame as soon as it is ripe, or divide carefully in spring, once the shoots are visible.

POPULAR SPECIES

R. cautleoides (China). This species has pale yellow flowers on leafy stems, in early summer. 23cm (9in).
R. purpurea (Himalaya). This species has purple flowers, in summer. 30cm (1ft).

Roscoea purpurea

S

SCHIZOSTYLIS
(Kaffir lily)

The name is derived from the Greek words *schizo* (split) and *stylos* (style), referring to the deeply divided style.

Schizostylis coccinea 'Major'

These rhizomatous perennials are especially useful because they flower so late in the season, sometimes at the approach of winter. They look best in mixed borders, in a sunny position in front of shrubs, provided the soil is not too dry.

The plants are not reliably hardy in cold areas, but usually survive with protection.

HOW TO GROW

Grow in a moist, fertile soil, but they will grow in ordinary soil if watered well in dry weather. Plant to a depth of 5cm (2in).

In cold areas, protect the roots with a thick layer of bracken or peat, held in place with netting, for the winter.

PROPAGATION

Divide the roots in mid spring, replanting small clusters of offsets.

POPULAR SPECIES

S. coccinea (South Africa). Narrow, sword-like foliage and loose spikes of pink or red flowers in mid and late autumn. 'Major' has large red flowers; 'Mrs Hegarty' is a popular pink variety. 60–90cm (2–3ft).

SCILLA

Scillas should always be on the shopping list. They are inexpensive, easy to grow, and because they can be left to naturalize and increase themselves, they have to be good value.

They are small, attractive plants with nodding blue bells, best seen in a dense group. They are excellent for planting in the rock garden, as a seasonal spring-flowering plant massed in containers or raised beds, or naturalized.

HOW TO GROW

Scillas do best in moist but well-drained ground. Plant in autumn about 5–8cm (2–3in) apart, covered with 5–8cm (2–3in) of soil. If naturalizing, it is a good idea simply to

Scilla peruviana 'Alba'

scatter them on the ground and plant them where they fall, to prevent the planting from looking too formal.

Left alone, they should continue to flower and multiply each year.

PROPAGATION

Lift an established clump as the leaves die down and remove some offset bulbs to replant. They will probably flower in one or two years.

Scilla bifolia

Alternatively sow seed once it ripens in early summer, in pots in a cold frame. Plant out the seedlings into a nursery bed at the end of the second year. It may take three to five years from sowing to flowering.

▼ *Scilla sibirica* 'Taurica'

▼ *Scilla tubergeniana*

Scilla sibirica 'Spring Beauty'

POPULAR SPECIES

S. bifolia (S. Europe to Turkey). Blue nodding starry flowers in late winter and early spring. 15cm (6in).

S. peruviana (Algeria, Italy). Dense heads of blue starry flowers, in late spring and early summer. 'Alba' is a white form. 23cm (9in).

S. sibirica (C. and S. Russia). Bright blue bell-shaped flowers in early spring. 'Spring Beauty' is a deeper blue. There is also an uncommon white form. 15cm (6in).

S. tubergeniana (Iran). Pale blue bells with a dark stripe down the centre of each petal. Late winter. 10cm (4in).

SPARAXIS

he name comes from the Greek word *sparasso*, meaning to tear, a reference to the lacerated spathes.

These delicate-looking cormous plants are not dependably hardy and winter losses can be expected if you leave them outside in cold regions. If you live in a cold area, try growing them in pots. You will find sparaxis offered in both autumn and spring bulb catalogues.

HOW TO GROW

In mild areas, plant outdoors in late autumn (earlier planting may increase the risk of frost damage), but in cold areas plant in early spring and lift the bulbs in autumn to store in a frost-free place. Plant the corms about 8cm (3in) deep and 5cm (2in) apart in well-drained soil in a sunny, sheltered spot.

The fine stems may need support unless being grown through other plants.

If growing in pots, plant about six corms in a 15cm (6in) pot, and keep in a cool greenhouse.

PROPAGATION

Remove the small cormlets when lifting the plants, and grow on in a cold frame. They should flower in about two years.

POPULAR SPECIES

S. tricolor hybrids (garden origin). The species itself is not grown but it is the colourful hybrids that are of garden value. The common name 'harlequin flower' refers to the vividly coloured flowers, which may be orange, red, pink, or purple, with black and yellow centres; early summer. 20cm (8in).

STERNBERGIA

These plants are named after Count Kaspar von Sternberg, an Austrian botanist.

Hardy bulbous plants that deserve to be better known, the sternbergias are especially worth buying because they add a touch of extra colour to autumn when it is most appreciated. The bulbs are not common in garden shops, but you will find them in most good bulb catalogues.

Resembling yellow crocuses, they flower when most other plants are finishing. They look best in a rock garden or at the front of a mixed or shrub border.

HOW TO GROW

Plant 10cm (4in) deep in late summer or early autumn, about the same distance apart, in well-drained soil in a sunny position.

Plant the bulbs in a group, and leave them undisturbed if possible.

Sternbergia clusiana

Sternbergia lutea

PROPAGATION

Remove and replant bulb offsets in late summer. They will often flower within two years.

POPULAR SPECIES

S. clusiana (Asia Minor). Yellow goblet-like flowers on short stems, in early and mid autumn, before the leaves appear. 10cm (4in).
S. lutea (E. Mediterranean, Iran). Yellow crocus-like flowers about 5cm (2in) long, in early and mid autumn. 13cm (5in).

T

TIGRIDIA
(Peacock flower, tiger flower)

These eyecatching tender plants have to be lifted each autumn, but they are worth the effort. The three large and colourful petals spread out from the cup to form a flower up to 15cm (6in) across. The throats are usually attractively spotted and blotched. The showy flowers last only a day, but they are soon replaced by others. They are attractive in an herbaceous or mixed border.

HOW TO GROW
Plant in mid spring, about 13cm (5in) apart, with about 5cm (2in) of soil over the bulb. A rich, sandy soil is best, but they also need plenty of moisture during the growing season. Give them a warm, sheltered position.

Lift the plants before severe frosts are likely, and store the bulbs in a frost-free place until spring. In mild areas they will survive outdoors for most winters.

Tigridia pavonia

PROPAGATION
Remove the offset bulbs and grow on in a cold frame or nursery bed (lifting and protecting them for the winter if necessary). The bulbs may take a year or two to reach flowering size.

POPULAR SPECIES
I. pavonia (Mexico, Peru). The highly bred strains that are sold have white, yellow, orange, scarlet, crimson, and rose, flowers, many of them bicoloured, summer to early autumn. 45cm (1½ft).

Tigridia pavonia

TULIPA

Tulips need no introduction. For centuries they have been among the most sought-after spring-flowering bulbs, and hybridists have achieved a remarkable range of colours and forms. And if you find the highly bred forms too stiff and artificial in appearance, there are plenty of worthwhile species tulips to try.

The genus takes its name from the Persian words *thoulyban* or *tulipant* or the Turkish word *tulband*, all meaning turban, referring to the shape of the tulip flower.

Because most tulips are narrow in profile, isolated or widely spaced plants seldom look

Tulipa 'Golden Harvest' (Cottage)

Tulipa 'General de Wet' (Single Early)

Tulipa 'Bellona' (Single Early)

△ *Tulipa* 'Apeldoorn' (Darwin Hybrid)

△ *Tulipa* 'Pink Beauty' (Single Early)

▽ *Tulipa* 'The Bishop' (Darwin)

▽ *Tulipa* 'Dutch Princess' (Mid Season)

▽ *Tulipa fosteriana* hybrid 'Purissima'

▽ *Tulipa* 'May Blossom' (Rembrandt)

Tulipa greigii hybrid 'Oriental Splendour'

Tulipa greigii hybrid 'Donna Bella'

effective. Plant tulips closely if you want to see them at their best. If using them for formal spring bedding, try interplanting tulips with spring bedding plants such as forget-me-nots, which bring colour closer to the ground and help to avoid the rather unattractive 'stalky' appearance of the taller kinds of tulips.

Single Early tulips are self-descriptive. They are often used for forcing, but are also good outdoors. Because of their short stature, they are good for beds and borders, in mid spring. 'Princess Irene' is a good orange variety. 25–40cm (10–16in).

Double Early tulips look like small peonies. They are compact and more

Tulipa greigii hybrid 'Gluck'

Tulipa greigii hybrid 'Plaisir'

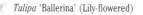

Tulipa greigii hybrid 'Red Riding Hood'

Tulipa 'China Pink' (Lily-flowered)

Tulipa greigii hybrid 'Cape Cod'

Tulipa 'Ballerina' (Lily-flowered)

▲ *Tulipa batalinii*

▼ *Tulipa saxatilis*

▲ *Tulipa kaufmanniana* hybrid 'The First'

▼ *Tulipa tarda*

suitable than the singles for containers and massed bedding in an exposed position, and are also good for forcing. They flower in mid spring. 'Orange Nassau' is a good orange-red variety. 25–40cm (10–16in).

The group often known as **May-flowering** tulips usually includes both Darwin tulips and Cottage tulips (both of which have egg-shaped flowers on long stems). They flower in late spring. 60–75cm (2–2½ft).

Darwin Hybrid tulips have some of the finest and largest flowers. They were created by crossing Darwins with *T. fosteriana.* They are slightly earlier than the ordinary Darwins, but the colour range is not so good. They flower in mid to late spring. 'Holland's Glory' is an outstanding poppy red. 60–75cm (2–2½ft).

Lily-flowered tulips have pointed petals, often reflexed, creating an upright lily shape; they flower in late spring. 'Westpoint' is an outstanding deep yellow. 45–60cm (1½–2ft).

Mid-season tulips have large flowers on strong, stiff stems, and flower at a time that conveniently bridges the gap between early-and May-flowering tulips. Their strong, sturdy habit makes them suitable for bedding in fairly exposed positions in the garden. 45–60cm (1½–2ft).

Parrot and fringed tulips have large flowers with long, twisted and cut or fringed petals, in late spring. They are easily damaged by bad weather but make very attractive cut flowers. 'Gay Presto' is one of the most colourful varieties, having red and white petals. 45–75cm (1½–2½ft).

Viridiflora tulips have a large proportion of green on the petals. They add interest to flower arrangements, but are not the boldest or brightest tulips for display in the garden. 'Angel', which is cream-white and green, has strong flower arranger appeal. 23–60cm (9–24in) high.

Rembrandt Tulips are Darwin tulips with 'broken' or variegated colouring, sometimes feathered, flowering in late spring. As this colour 'breaking' may be caused by a virus, it is best not to plant them with other kinds. 60–75cm (2–2½ft) high.

Tulipa praestans 'Fusilier'

Tulipa 'Aladdin' (Lily-flowered)

Tulipa praestans

Tulipa 'Flaming Parrot' (Parrot)

Tulipa 'Peach Blossom' (Double Early)

HOW TO GROW

Plant outdoors in full sun or partial shade in mid or late autumn, about 15cm (6in) deep and 8–15cm (3–6in) apart; increase the distance if being interplanted with spring bedding plants. Tulips prefer a sandy loam, and do well on alkaline soils. Dead-head as the first petals fall.

As tulips seldom flower well the second year (except some of the species), it is best to lift the bulbs once the foliage is turning yellow. Dry off and store until planting time again. The largest bulbs may flower again, but the smaller offsets may have to be grown on in a nursery bed for a couple of years before they reach flowering size.

Tulipa 'Orange Nassau' (Double Early)

Tulipa 'Texas Gold' (Parrot)

Tulipa 'Mount Tacoma' (Double Late)

Many of the species are best left undisturbed, especially if they are grown in a rock garden.

Many ordinary varieties can be forced into early flowering indoors, but the timing and methods can vary from variety to variety, so consult a specialist catalogue first if you want to try this.

Tulipa kaufmanniana hybrid 'Franz Lehar'

Tulipa kaufmanniana hybrid 'Show-winner'

Tulipa 'Stockholm' (Double Early)

PROPAGATION

Separate and grow on the offsets as described above.

POPULAR SPECIES

T. batalinii (Bokhara). Buff-yellow flowers in late spring; there are also varieties with apricot and sulphuryellow flushed with

Tulipa 'Angelique' (Double Late)

orange flowers. 13cm (5in) high.

T. fosteriana hybrids (C. Asia). Usually big scarlet flowers with blunt-pointed petals, in mid spring. 'Madame Lefeber' (also known as 'Red Emperor') is a famous bright scarlet variety. 30–45cm (1–1½ft).

T. greigii hybrids (C. Asia). Variegated foliage. The flowers are large for the height of the plant, and there are several colours; in late spring. 'Red Riding Hood' is a famous variety with boldly blotched foliage and dazzling scarlet flowers. 23cm (9in).

T. kaufmanniana hybrids (Turkestan). Known as the waterlily tulip. The pointed buds open out into a fairly flat open 'lily' shape. They are among the earliest tulips to

Tulipa 'Mr Van der Hoef' (Double Early)   *Tulipa* 'Electra' (Double Early)

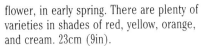

Tulipa fosteriana 'Purissima'

Tulipa fosteriana 'Red Emperor'

flower, in early spring. There are plenty of varieties in shades of red, yellow, orange, and cream. 23cm (9in).

T. praestans (C. Asia). Unlike most tulips, this one produces clusters of several flowers on each stalk. 'Fusilier', with flaming scarlet flowers which bloom in early or mid spring,

is one of the best. 30cm (1ft).

T. saxatilis (Crete). Pink flowers with yellow centres, in spring. 30cm (1ft).

T. tarda (C. Asia). An outstanding species for the rock garden. Clusters of star-like yellow and white flowers in early spring. 13cm (5in) high.

Tulipa fosteriana 'Princeps'

Tulipa fosteriana 'Cantata'

Z

ZANTEDESCHIA

he genus is named after Francesco Zantedeschi, an Italian botanist.
These rhizomatous plants have very distinctive 'flowers'; the proper flowers are actually insignificant because they are set in a large white or coloured spathe typical of the arum lilies. Unfortunately they are not dependably hardy. In Britain they are popularly known as arum lilies, and in the USA as calla lilies. Zantedeschias are best grown in large pots in a greenhouse or conservatory, but *Z. aethiopica* can be grown outdoors in mild areas.

HOW TO GROW

Plant in early spring, covering the rhizome

Zantedeschia aethiopica

with about 5–8cm (2–3in) of compost. Keep just moist until growth appears, then water freely. Feed weekly in summer, and gradually withhold water again in autumn. If growing outdoors, start off indoors and plunge the pot outdoors for the summer. If leaving the plant outdoors it will probably need some winter protection even in mild areas.

PROPAGATION

Divide the rhizome or remove offsets when repotting.

POPULAR SPECIES

Z. aethiopica (South Africa). Known as the white arum lily; it has big white spathes surrounding a conspicuous yellow spadix, in mid spring and early June. 'Crowborough' is a relatively hardy form. 60–90cm (2–3ft).
Z. elliottiana (South Africa). Spotted heart-shaped leaves; yellow spathes, mid spring to early summer. 60cm (2ft).
Z. rehmannii (South Africa). Leaves sometimes flecked silvery-white, small pink to red spathes, in late spring. There is also a white form. 30cm (1ft).

ZEPHYRANTHES

hese delicate-looking tender plants take their name from the Greek words *zephyros* (the west wind) and *anthos* (flower), alluding to the western hemisphere, from where these plants originate. They are sometimes known as the flowers of the west wind. Zephyr lily and fairy lily are other common names.

They can be grown outdoors in the summer but are generally best in a greenhouse or conservatory. Because of their small size they are best planted in groups.

HOW TO GROW

Outdoors, plant in spring, in a sunny spot, preferably in a sandy soil. Plant the bulbs about 5cm (2in) apart and cover with about 3cm (1in) of soil. Lift the bulbs in the autumn and store them in a frost-free place until the following spring. Grow in pots under glass.

PROPAGATION

Separate offsets in spring and grow on (lifting each autumn) until flowering size is reached.

POPULAR SPECIES

Z. candida (Argentina, Uruguay). White flowers with bright yellow anthers, above grass-like foliage. 15cm (6in).
Z. grandiflora (S. Mexico, Guatemala). Large pink flowers. 23cm (6in).

Zephyranthes candida

Zephyranthes grandiflora

ACKNOWLEDGEMENTS

The publishers would like to thank the following individuals and organizations for supplying photographs: A–Z Collection, B. Alfieri, G. Beckett, Biofotos, Pat Brindley, J. Cowley, Iris Hardwick, A. Huxley, Peter McHoy, Tania Midgley, Ray Proctor, K. Scowen, Harry Smith Collection, Michael Warren.